I Saw Satan Fall Like Lightning

A Divine Revelation of How to Take New Authority Over the Devil

Sue Curran

CREATION HOUSE
Orlando, FL

I SAW SATAN FALL LIKE LIGHTNING by Sue Curran
Published by Creation House
Strang Communications Company
600 Rinehart Road
Lake Mary, Florida 32746
Web site: http://www.creationhouse.com

Unless otherwise noted, all Scripture quotations are from the King
James Version of the Bible.

Scripture quotations marked NIV are from the Holy Bible, New
International Version. Copyright © 1973, 1978, 1984, International Bible
Society. Used by permission.

Library of Congress Cataloging-in-Publication Data:
Curran, Sue.
        I saw Satan fall like lightening / Sue Curran.
            p. cm.
        Includes bibliographical references.
        ISBN: 0–88419–546–5 (pbk.)
        1. Devil. 2. Spiritual warfare. 3. Spiritual life—Christianity.
    I. Title.
BT981.C87 1998
235'.47—dc21   98-13826
                                                         CIP

89012345 BBG 87654321
Printed in the United States of America

DEDICATION

Dedicated to my husband, John, who has loved me, supported me, and released me into the full scope of the ministry call that God has placed upon my life.

ACKNOWLEDGMENTS

I wish to acknowledge the faithful support and encouragement of my dear friend, Fuchsia Pickett. I would also like to thank Carol Noe for her help in organizing the material and her suggestions for clarity of presentation. My deep appreciation goes to my prayer partners at Shekinah Church for persevering with me in prayer concerning this book.

CONTENTS

ONE

REVELATION OF AUTHORITY

W E ARE LIVING in a *breakthrough hour.* It is a different season on God's sovereign timetable than we have ever known. Christian leaders are calling today the "wonder years of world evangelization." Some missiologists and church-growth experts believe it is quite possible that more souls could come to Christ between now and the end of this century than in all of recorded church history.[1]

As I have read reports of the tremendous increase in the number of Christians throughout the world in recent years, it has almost taken my breath. According to many reports we are living in a time of unprecedented growth for the kingdom of God. For example, in 1900 only 9 percent of Africa professed to be Christian; it is projected that at the current growth rate, 48 percent of the entire African population will be born-again Christians by the end of this century.[2]

Before the turn of this century, Korea had no Christian witness and was declared "impossible to penetrate" by its missionaries. Now, 30 percent of that nation are born-again Christians.[3] It is projected that if Koreans continue to convert to Christianity at the present rate, 60 percent of Korea will be born again by the year 2000![4] And in South America the church has continued to grow dramatically as well. For example, the church in Argentina has grown more in the last four years than it did in the previous one hundred years.[5]

When we consider the growth of Christianity historically, today's statistical growth appears even more phenomenal. In A.D. 100 there were three hundred sixty non-Christians for every true believer—a ratio of three hundred sixty to one. Today that ratio of non-Christians to believers is seven to one.[6] Even calculating the non-Christian to Christian ratio from 1900 to today, the contrast is incredible. In 1900 there were fifteen unbelievers born for every person who was born again, a ratio of fifteen to one. In 1992 there were two people born for every person who was born again, a ratio of two to one.[7]

During my intense studies of the background of this growth explosion, I heard an evangelist speak who gave me the key to a wonderful, life-changing discovery that is the "seed thought" for this book. Carlos Annacondia, Argentina's leading layevangelist, is credited with winning over a million souls to the Lord in less than four years in the country of Argentina. He leads an average of one thousand people a day to a public commitment to Christ.[8] Like Dwight Moody of an earlier century, Annacondia is not an ordained minister, but a layperson who, by his fruitful life, is proving that God will use whomever He chooses. Some say he is the greatest evangelist living today. Wisdom dictates that we listen carefully to what a man with such fruitfulness in the kingdom has to say.

Hearing Carlos Annacondia speak one sentence changed forever the way I view the spiritual battle for souls in which we are involved. In fact, his startling statement sent me studying and searching the Scriptures for greater understanding of this wonderful truth. What I subsequently discovered during my study became a "eureka" element in my spiritual life. It has set me on a journey that has resulted in a new, more effective realm of prayer in my life and ministry. But it was what God spoke to Carlos Annacondia that became a revelatory key for me, unlocking a greater dimension of the power of prayer and the authority we have over the enemy and dramatically changing my life and ministry.

How could one statement have such an effect on my life? It came to my heart as a thread that, when pulled in the light of new revelation from the Word, began to unravel wonderful truths that have been life changing. Annacondia explained the revelation of one divine principle that was the single element in his own heart that propelled him into his present fruitful ministry. It came to him as he was praying earnestly that God would give him more power to be able to heal the sick and win souls. As he continued to cry out in great fervency of heart for this divine power, he heard God speak clearly to him: "You do not need more power; you need to release the authority I have given you."

As many of us so often do, Annacondia was asking sincerely and in faith for greater victory and fruitfulness in his life. However, unknowingly, he was seeking the wrong ingredient to bring him that victory. In spite of his misdirected prayer, the Holy Spirit faithfully spoke to his seeking heart what he really needed. It was not more *power* that he needed. He simply needed to learn to release the *authority* he had been given.

How many times have we looked at our own lives and churches and lamented over the fact that we have too little power to win souls to Christ? We have thought we needed more divine power to accomplish the formidable task of bringing people to salvation. According to the revelation the Lord gave to Annacondia, however, it is not *power* we need to see souls come to the Lord, but a *release of the divine authority we have been given.*

As I allowed that word to stir my spirit, and as I began to search the Scriptures, I could see how very accurate this revelatory word was to Annacondia. To gain the victory Christ intended us to have in our Christian lives, and to win others to Christ, what we need is the understanding of how to release our authority—the authority we have been given through Christ's work on Calvary and by His divine commission.

THE DISCIPLES' COMMISSIONS

MY HEART SO responded to the idea of learning to release our authority that, as I went to the Scriptures again to see what they had to teach about authority, a wonderful reality began to leap out of one verse after another, clarifying to me what Jesus said when He gave His disciples their divine commissions.

Jesus called His disciples to him and declared: "Behold, I give unto you power . . . over all the power of the enemy: and nothing shall by any means hurt you" (Luke 10:19). It is unfortunate that the King James translation does not give the clarity we need to understand this divine commission. In the original Greek this verse does not read that Jesus gave them "power . . . over all the power," but that He gave them "authority (Greek—*exousia*) over power (Greek—*dunamis*)." A more accurate translation of that verse from the Greek, then, is: "I have given you *authority* . . . to overcome all the *power* of the enemy; nothing will harm you" (Luke 10:19, NIV, emphasis added).

AUTHORITY VS. POWER

AS WE BEGIN to understand the crucial difference between the *authority* Jesus has given us and the *power* of the enemy, we will experience a dramatic change in our effectiveness in prayer and in our results in building the kingdom. When we lay hold of the reality of our divine authority that prevails over the power of the enemy, we enter a greater realm of spiritual understanding where we can experience the ultimate victory that Jesus intended for us as believers and for His church corporately.

4

After first commissioning His twelve disciples, Jesus later sent out seventy-two others who returned with joy and said, "Lord, even the demons submit to us in your name" (Luke 10:17–18, NIV). Seemingly unimpressed, Jesus responded, "I saw Satan fall like lightning from heaven. I have given you authority to trample on snakes and scorpions and to overcome all the power of the enemy; nothing will harm you" (Luke 10:18, NIV). When Jesus commissioned these disciples, He gave them *authority* to overcome all the *power* of the enemy. He explained that the demons were subject to them because He had given them authority over all the devil's power.

AUTHORITY DEFINED

NOT UNDERSTANDING the authority we have been given as believers, many of us have thought that in order to be victorious over the enemy of our lives, we needed more power. The truth is that we simply need to understand the authority we have been given!

Authority can be defined as "permission or right that is given to another by one who has the authority to do so." *Power* can be defined simply as "ability." Through Christ's victory at Calvary, every believer has been given the *permission and the right* to rule over the existing power of the devil. *Authority* means we may do it, we have a right to do it, and we are equipped to do it. Walking in this reality of the authority we have been given is the missing element for many Christians who have felt defeated because they thought they lacked power to do the "greater works" that Jesus promised we would do.

Although the Scriptures do refer to the "power of the enemy," we need to realize that he has only limited power. We will investigate the source and limitations of his power later in our study. Because he is a spirit being, however, his power can seem greater than our human power. If we endeavor to fight him using power against power, we will surely experience a continual battle that will lead us to frustration and ultimate defeat. We shall see how learning to release the authority Jesus gave us over Satan's power paralyzes his ability to operate and sets us free from that continuing struggle, bringing us the victory we desire.

Though the devil has limited power, he has no *legitimate authority* to exercise that power. According to the Scriptures, Jesus crushed Satan's head and gained the authority over all principalities and powers. "And having spoiled principalities and powers, he made a shew of them openly, triumphing over them in it" (Col. 2:15). Since this is true, what is the ongoing battle that we have to fight as Christians in order to have our lives established in God and to bring others into the kingdom? The controversy we face is based in the issue of authority, not power. Our victory as believers does not have to do with who has the greater power—the devil or Christians—but with who has and will ultimately exercise true authority.

AUTHORITY ILLUSTRATED

RECENTLY, I WAS accosted by a traffic policeman. I had not had that wonderful experience for many years. I had to admit to exceeding the speed limit, which was posted as fifteen miles per hour in the state park near our home. I was going to play a quick game of tennis, and on my way I realized I had forgotten to make a phone call. Hurrying along, absorbed in my busy schedule, I was thinking about where to make the phone call before my partner arrived for the tennis match.

As I pulled into a parking place near a phone booth in the park, a patrolman pulled in behind me. He got out of his car and walked toward me. I still did not realize my guilt, so I greeted him happily: "Hello, Officer." When I realized I was the object of his visit, it occurred to me that maybe he had heard me preach on Sunday and wanted to chat. (After I found out what he wanted, I didn't mention preaching or make any admissions to being a minister.)

He responded gruffly to my greeting, "Do you know what the speed limit is in the park?" You know how intimidating a policeman's tone of voice can be.

"Yes, sir, I do."

He was startled. He barked out, "You *know* what the speed limit is?"

I said, "Yes, sir, and I'm sorry. I'm sure I must have been exceeding the limit."

He scowled, "You certainly were."

I said, "Well, I thank you for calling that to my attention."

Finally, in a more civil tone he said, "Well, I tell you what; I don't want to ruin your day. So I am going to give you a warning this time. Now, you take it easy, will you?"

And I said, "Oh, I will, and you have done me a favor today."

"Well," he retorted, his tone still gruff, "we don't want anybody to get hurt around here."

This happily resolved incident with the local police served as a catalyst to my study of the basis of authority. If I had realized that a police officer was following me that day in the park, I could have gunned my engine and outrun him for a while. But what would have been the point? He would have radioed to someone else who had the same authority as he did and enlisted their help to subdue me. All I would have done by resisting his authority would have been to bring greater condemnation upon myself. So I might as well yield my limited power in the face of such authority. In my case, the lines of authority were established by the state of Tennessee's state parks association and the city of Kingsport's law enforcement agency.

They had determined that this officer had the authority to prosecute me for violation of the law. Even the fact that I pray every day could not negate my paying the consequences of violating that authority. The officer had been given jurisdiction in certain areas to exercise his authority over anyone who violated them.

When someone has been given authority, it doesn't matter that another comes to try to exercise his power to resist that authority. Such resistance will only result in continued injury to the one attacking the authority of the other. The more resistance that is created, the higher the realm of authority that will be invoked to subdue that resistance.

ALL AUTHORITY BELONGS TO CHRIST

IN THIS WAY, the realm of authority we have been given as Christians is directly related to the authority of Christ—the One who gave it. When Jesus commissioned His disciples, He declared: "*All* authority in heaven and on earth has been given to me" (Matt. 28:18, NIV, emphasis added). What are the limits to the jurisdiction of our authority according to this declaration? What does it mean to have *all* authority? Understanding the answers to these questions will wonderfully increase our effectiveness in fulfilling the Great Commission.

Two

Authority of
the Great Commission

A N ACCURATE UNDERSTANDING of the words of Jesus that we
call the "Great Commission" will help us walk in the
reality of the divine authority that has been given us.

> And Jesus came and spake unto them, saying, All power
> is given unto me in heaven and in earth. Go ye there-
> fore, and teach all nations, baptizing them in the name
> of the Father, and of the Son, and of the Holy Ghost:
> Teaching them to observe all things whatsoever I have
> commanded you: and, lo, I am with you alway, even
> unto the end of the world. Amen.
>
> —MATTHEW 28:18–20

Jesus followed His declaration, "All power is given unto
me," by saying, "Go ye *therefore*." Anytime we see the word
therefore in the Scriptures it is good to ask ourselves, "What is
it there for?" There is a direct causal relationship between the
reality of Jesus having been given all power and His imme-
diate command to us to go fulfill the Great Commission.

The Obedience Factor

THE GREEK WORD translated *power* here is *exousia,* which we have seen actually means "authority." So in essence Jesus was saying to His disciples, "All *authority* has been given to Me, therefore you have *authority* to go fulfill My commission to you." His command came with the divine equipping we need to fulfill it, as only God's commands can do.

To receive a commission is one thing; to successfully carry it to completion is quite another. Many sincere believers who have read Jesus' commission have tried to obey by going out to reap the harvest without success. Why? What was the reason for their ineffectiveness? Was Jesus' commission for the first disciples only? Is His power not the same today as it was then? Surely we must respond with a resounding *no* to these questions. Jesus' commission is for all who follow Him in obedience, and His power is unchanging for all eternity.

To what, then, do we attribute the dismal failure of sincere Christians to walk in victory in their personal lives? What causes their ineffectiveness in bringing souls to Christ? I am convinced that the unsuccessful efforts of many to fulfill Jesus' commission are due to the fact that they have gone out without first understanding how to release the authority for the task to which they have been commissioned. They have been unaware of the divine equipping they have received for the task.

How exciting must Jesus' promises have been to the disciples in retrospect as they rejoiced in the presence of the resurrected Christ! They must have remembered His words to them before His death and marveled at His wonderful provision. He was very clear about their commission as well as the source of their ability to carry it out. He would give them all they needed to fulfill His Great Commission.

Promise of Power

But ye shall receive power, after that the Holy Ghost is

come upon you: and ye shall be witnesses unto me both in Jerusalem, and in all Judaea, and in Samaria, and unto the uttermost part of the earth.

—ACTS 1:8

Jesus had promised His disciples a baptism of *dunamis*—divine power—when the Holy Ghost would come. They were to wait in the upper room until the Holy Spirit came to give them His supernatural power. Receiving the baptism of the Holy Spirit according to Acts 1:8 gives us the *dunamis* of the Holy Spirit—that wonderful supernatural power to be His witnesses. Without this supernatural empowering, we cannot hope to fulfill the Great Commission. That promise is a vital part of Christ's provision for all believers.

However, many have received the baptism of the Holy Spirit and yet have not seen the Great Commission fulfilled in their lives. Along with this reality of divine power, this supernatural *dunamis* given us by the infilling of the Holy Spirit, Christ has also given us *exousia*—divine authority—over all the power of the enemy. Understanding and giving ourselves to the reality of this latter provision will bring the effectiveness to our lives that we so desperately need. It is foundational to the message of the gospel, and yet we have missed it so tragically.

PROPHETIC REVELATION OF RESTORED AUTHORITY

And I will put enmity between thee and the woman, and between thy seed and her seed; it shall bruise thy head, and thou shalt bruise his heel.

—GENESIS 3:15

In the Book of Genesis, when the first promise of Redemption is given, the Bible declares that Jesus would one day bruise Satan's head (Gen. 3:15). The Hebrew word for *bruise* literally means "to crush." The promise to crush Satan's head indicates a destruction of his headship or authority.

That is exactly what Jesus finally accomplished through His death on the cross. With Satan's authority crushed, Jesus regained His legitimate headship over mankind. Any tyranny the devil still exercises comes strictly from the serpent's writhing in his death struggle. Though his head is crushed, his body can still wiggle around and terrify men and women who do not recognize the death struggle.

To the degree that a believer submits to the lordship of Jesus Christ, that believer will gain a greater degree of victory over the enemy. The apostle James instructed believers to "submit yourselves therefore to God. Resist the devil, and he will flee from you" (James 4:7). I began to see in my study that complete abandonment to the lordship of Christ gives us complete jurisdiction of authority over the devil.

Carlos Annacondia did not understand this place of authority when he prayed, "Power, Lord, give me power. I want to heal the sick. I want to cast out devils. You said that You would give us power. I'm asking You, Lord, for the power."

When the Lord finally said to him, "Quit asking for power; what you need is to release the authority I have given you," Annacondia entered into a new realm of understanding his authority and a new effectiveness in ministry.[1]

After hearing the Lord speak that startling statement to him, Annacondia went to a hospital to pray for the sick and to release the authority that the Lord had given to him. As he approached the first patient, he said, "May I pray for you in Jesus' name?"

The person responded, "I'm a Catholic; don't bother me." (Unfortunately, in South America many evangelicals and Catholics do not get along.)

Annacondia went from bed to bed asking, "May I pray for you in Jesus' name that you can be healed?"

The response was always, "I am Catholic; don't bother me." Annacondia continued to approach patients until he had gone to forty-nine beds, each of whom had flatly refused his offer for prayer. It takes a good measure of faith to endure that much rejection. When he approached the fiftieth bed the woman lying there looked at him and said rather brusquely, "I have nothing to lose, why not? Go ahead, pray." The woman was a cripple. Carlos Annacondia laid hands on her and simply spoke her healing in the authority of Jesus' name. Immediately, she jumped out of the bed and began to walk.

The people all around started shouting, *"Milagro, milagro* (Miracle, miracle)!" And then the people began to charge him, begging him to pray for them.[2]

Many people were healed in the hospital that day as Annacondia simply responded in obedience to the new revelation of the authority he had been given in the name of Jesus.

The only thing that had changed for Annacondia as he went to the hospital that day was that he had heard the Lord tell him not to ask for power, but to release the authority he already had. In simple faith and obedience, he went with this key to victory and prayed for the sick with miraculous results. Today he is walking in a realm of authority that enables him to take entire cities for Christ. He is now winning thousands of people to the Lord.

How many souls will we win to the Lord once we grasp the reality that Annacondia grasped by faith through what the Lord spoke to him? He discovered that the key to fulfilling the Great Commission is to release the authority Christ has given us. As we determine to walk in obedience to the divine mandate Christ left us, we will learn to command authority over the powers of darkness that keep men from coming to Christ.

OBEDIENCE: THE BASIS FOR AUTHORITY

When Jesus was entered into Capernaum, there came unto him a centurion, beseeching him, and saying, Lord, my servant lieth at home sick of the palsy, grievously tormented. And Jesus saith unto him, I will come and heal him. The centurion answered and said, Lord, I am not worthy that thou shouldest come under my roof: but speak the word only, and my servant shall be healed. For I am a man under authority, having soldiers under me: and I say to this man, Go, and he goeth; and to another, Come, and he cometh; and to my servant, Do this, and he doeth it. When Jesus heard it, he marvelled, and said to them that followed, Verily I say unto you, I have not found so great faith, no, not in Israel.

—Matthew 8:5–10

Obedience is the basis for walking in authority. Though this may seem to be an obvious fact, it cannot be overstated. While some Christians may have been disappointed in their fruitless efforts to fulfill the Great Commission, they have at least answered the call of obedience to go. Those who refuse the call to go will never know the authority God has given them because they have not obeyed this simple command of Jesus. Of course, when we refer to obeying the call to "go" we are not speaking of going around the world to a mission field, necessarily. Perhaps our obedience will only require us to go to people we meet every day who do not know Jesus Christ. But we must determine to obey Jesus' commission fully—wherever it leads us.

If we expect to walk in divine authority over the power of the enemy, we have to first of all surrender in obedience to the authority of God over our lives. It is in that place of obedience that faith is born. Jesus witnessed to that reality when the centurion came to Him, asking Him to heal his servant. It is clear from the man's own declaration that he understood the power of words when they were spoken by a man under authority. He was saying to Jesus that he understood authority because he was a man *under* authority.

Jesus did not marvel at his understanding or wisdom, but at his *faith*. It was the faith of one who understood the reality of authority because he was himself obedient to authority. Faith that comes to our hearts through obedience

14

cannot be denied, because "we know that we know" that what we have declared is ours. The centurion understood he was submitted to another in obedience, which submission gave him authority to command those under him. Having walked in that authority, he understood the power of the spoken word to command obedience to that delegated authority.

On another occasion Jesus taught the principle of authority through obedience when He asked the question: "And if ye have not been faithful in that which is another man's, who shall give you that which is your own?" (Luke 16:12). Until we are willing to live under authority, we can never under-stand authority in such a way that we can operate in it. If we do not submit our lives to the lordship of Christ and yield to His will, even though we might make heaven as a born-again believer, we will never enjoy the victory that comes from walking in authority on the earth as Jesus promised us.

The Lord has a plan for His church to understand how authority is released through obedience. One reason some Christians do not experience this fresh anointing of joy that is being poured out on the church now is that their motive for receiving it is not correct. They want a new anointing to fulfill their own ministries and make them appear suc-cessful. They are more concerned for the success of their ministry than they are with obedience to the will of God. Jesus Christ is looking for people through whom He can pour His anointing and who are submitted to His lordship in the daily living of their lives. The anointing God gives is for the purpose of accomplishing His will, not for the fulfill-ment of our ministries as some have mistakenly thought. Our obedience to His will is the key to releasing His divine anointing throughout our lives.

The only way we can operate in the authority that God intended is to understand that we must live first of all under God's authority. We have been sent to do His will in the earth, as Jesus was sent to do His Father's will. Jesus declared that He came not to do His own will, but the will of His Father (John 5:30). And after His Resurrection, He said to His disciples, "As my Father hath sent me, even so send I you" (John 20:21). When we grasp the vital relationship between our *obedience* to the will of God and the *power of the Word,* we too will be able to walk as men and women with authority over all the power of the enemy.

THREE

THE PATTERN SON: ESTABLISHING THE PATTERN

I T IS IMPERATIVE that we understand how Jesus could do the works that He did on earth as the Son of Man. Though He is the Son of God, He emptied Himself of His divinity when He came to earth as a man and did not use His divine prerogatives. He fulfilled all of His ministry as a Spirit-filled man. If we don't believe this, we will always think that Jesus was able to do miracles because He is God, and, of course, God does miracles. According to Paul's description of our Lord in the second chapter of Philippians, Jesus laid aside His deity and became a man; He walked as a servant of men. As a man, He was baptized in the Holy Spirit and empowered by the Spirit of God to do the will of the Father, just as you and I are.

ESTABLISHING HIS AUTHORITY

THROUGH THE EXAMPLE of how He lived His life, Jesus gave us the pattern of a Spirit-filled man walking in the anointing of the Holy Spirit with the divine ability to release captives and set them free. The Scriptures tell us clearly that Jesus came up out of the wilderness full of the Holy Ghost (Luke 4). Jesus Himself declared, "The Spirit of the Lord is upon me, because he hath anointed me . . . " (Luke 4:18). Jesus, the Son of man, a *Spirit-filled man,* demonstrated His intention for us to walk in obedience and victory through the anointing of the Holy Spirit on this earth.

As the pattern Son, Jesus showed us what it is like to walk in the authority of God through obedience to the Holy Spirit. It is through this understanding that we are going to step into a completely different world of fruitfulness in building the kingdom. There are three primary events in Jesus' life that establish for us a pattern for walking in divine authority. We witness this divine pattern first in His *wilderness temptation,* secondly in His agony in *Gethsemane,* and thirdly in His *Crucifixion* on Calvary. In each of these situations Jesus confronted temptation and evil and overcame the enemy completely through His obedience. By doing so He fulfilled the eternal plan of God and established a pattern of victorious living for us.

THE WILDERNESS

IMMEDIATELY AFTER HIS baptism in the Holy Spirit, Jesus was required to go into the wilderness. Through Jesus' declaration, "It is written," He gained the victory over the enemy in that terrible place of temptation. Satan could not withstand the authority of the Word of God. When Jesus said, "It is written, that man shall not live by bread alone," and again, "It is said, Thou shalt not tempt the Lord thy God," the tempter had to bow to the authority of the Word (Luke 4:4, 12). Jesus withstood the evil one simply by declaring the Word of God. On that authority He established His earthly ministry.

THE AUTHORITY OF THE WORD OF GOD

HOW DID JESUS do such miraculous works while He was on

the earth? He did them according to the Word of God. He declared who God's Word said He was and what God's Word said He was going to do. Jesus dramatically demonstrated the authority of that Word in the final scene of the wilderness temptation. After Satan had presented his evil temptations, Jesus said to him, "Get thee hence, Satan: for it is written, Thou shalt worship the Lord thy God, and him only shalt thou serve" (Matt. 4:10).

The next sentence is quite amazing: "Then the devil leaveth him" (Matt. 4:11). Jesus had the authority to tell the devil to get lost. The Scriptures do not record another instance of the devil confronting Jesus directly again. Though the enemy endeavored to work indirectly through a demoniac, or by causing a storm out at sea, there is no further record that he ever challenged Jesus personally in the verbal way he had accosted Him in the wilderness.

The pattern Jesus set for us here establishes as our basis of authority the written Word of God. If we are going to launch out and accomplish anything in the kingdom of God, our foundation—the place of beginning—must be the authority that He has given us through the Word of God. It is God's Word that gives authority over the power of the devil. When that authority was proven to be established in Jesus' life, He dismissed the devil. Think of it! When we come to a place of faith in the authority of the Word of God, we can overcome the worst temptations of the devil—and then dismiss him!

I think that one of the shortcomings of the Charismatic movement was all the construed "hand-to-hand combat" with the devil where believers tried to rebuke him and bind him in every unpleasant situation. As one sincere Christian testified, "The devil has been after me all day, praise His holy name." That may be simply an amusing misplacement of pronouns, but there is some truth in the faulty theology it reveals that many have unconsciously adopted.

The devil isn't after anyone all day long. It is important for us to understand that the devil is not omnipresent. He is one spirit being—just one. As such, he cannot be everywhere at one time. And most of us aren't going to become the devil's personal target.

The Wiles of the Devil

According to the Scriptures, Satan's primary ways of working are through *temptation, accusation,* and *deception. Temptation, the first way he chooses to work, can be seen in the temptation of Adam and Eve.* It is the classic picture of his skill as a tempter. He *tempts* to sin because he does not have the power to actually *make* anyone sin. He must have our consent to his temptation before he can cause us to sin. In the wilderness, Jesus defeated this work of the tempter and gave us a pattern for establishing our authority by standing on and proclaiming God's Word.

How does Satan use temptation to undermine our authority? At times he is successful simply because we do not recognize his work as a temptation. For example, I know that God's Word builds my faith in the authority of God. But if Satan can tempt me to be lazy or distracted so that I neglect the study of God's Word, then he can successfully undermine the authority I have in God. If I agree with Satan and do not discipline myself to read the Word, then I will be robbed of my authority by yielding to his temptation.

The devil's second means of working is through accusation. The Scriptures call him the "accuser of our brethren" who accused them before our God day and night (Rev. 12:10). The power in Satan's accusations is real. He can accuse me through insinuations that come as my own thoughts, even to the extent that they form strongholds in my mind. Or he can accuse through the words of people and, sadly, even the words of Christians.

But in order for Satan's accusations to do me harm, I must *receive* them. If I receive these words of accusation, they will defeat me through discouragement or fear and cause me to lose confidence. To overcome Satan's accusations, I must choose to refuse them entrance into my mind, emotions, and spirit. Satan has no authority to torment me with accusations. I can choose to resist him and maintain my place of authority as I refuse to yield the ground to him.

Though the Pharisees accused Jesus relentlessly, He refuted their arguments with the Word of God, receiving none of their lies against His character. We need to be alerted to the tactic of accusation, used by the devil, especially in the church, where it's become commonplace to hear someone leveling an accusation at a brother or sister. An accusing tongue is never the work of the Holy Spirit and must be resisted for the satanic work that it is.

Thirdly, Satan accomplishes his work through deception—by trying to deceive even the very elect if it were possible. His deadly half-truths are aimed at the heart of believers to entice them into error and deadly deception. He can be successful in deceiving us if we are willing to listen to his suggestions when they oppose God's truth. Many Christians have lost their place of authority because they simply do not stand on the Word of God. They do not insist that all that they allow in thought and deed line up with the Word of God.

People can be easily deceived if they have no spiritual covering in their lives. They have no one to bring them to accountability to God's Word and His way. Any of us can be deceived. We need to realize that deception is a tool of the enemy and place ourselves where we are not unnecessarily subjected to his attack. Once we are deceived, Satan is again empowered as he undermines our authority. God's authority must always be based on the truth of God's Word, and it cannot operate where deception has stolen the truth.

As we determine to love the truth, Satan's darts will fall powerless at our feet. Though men tried to make Jesus the king of an earthly kingdom, He refused to be deceived into turning from His divine mission—one that ultimately would make Him King of kings eternally. Though He was born to be King, Jesus could never accept the half-truth of a temporal kingdom as the deceiver wished He would do. It is wonderful to read the end of the Book and see that the devil's work as the deceiver ends when he is "cast into the bottomless pit . . . that he should deceive the nations no more" (Rev. 20:3).

Temptation, accusation, and deception are merely seductive works of the enemy that give him power only if we respond to his suggestions.

In a later chapter, we will discuss the fact that Satan has no legitimate power of his own—only what we give him by cooperating with his seductions through temptation, accusation, or deception.

THE PURPOSE OF JESUS' VICTORY

THE SCRIPTURES TEACH that Jesus came to destroy the works of the evil one (1 John 3:8). That is a powerful statement, one that we dare not ignore or disbelieve. The word *destroy* in the Greek is *luo,* which means "to loosen or cause to dissolve or come apart." Jesus came to divide and to cause to fall apart everything that the enemy is trying to build.

I like the illustration of the devil's attempt to sew a destructive garment, unaware that there is no thread in his bobbin. Though he works furiously, without the bobbin thread everything he thinks he has sewn together unravels at the seams. The Lord will always cause the work of the enemy to unravel before us as we walk in obedience and stand in our rightful authority.

When the enemy tries to work through a group of people in a church to cause a faction or a split, the saints can pray fervently on the authority of the Word and cause that destructive work of the devil to disintegrate before their eyes. Through our believing prayers, it is as if the breath of God were blowing on the devil's scheme and bringing it to nothing. That is the manifest authority of God brought to bear on an evil situation through obedience in prayer and declaration of the Word.

JESUS' AUTHORITY ESTABLISHED

AFTER JESUS DISMISSED the devil, angels came and ministered to Him. When Jesus came out of the wilderness, He immediately began to set people free from the tyranny of the devil. Matthew quoted the prophet Isaiah, saying, "The people living in darkness have seen a great light; on those living in the land of the shadow of death a light has dawned," acknowledging the fulfillment of that wonderful promise (Matt. 4:16, NIV).

The people in the area surrounding the place where Jesus delivered the demoniac began to be set free from their captivity to sin and sickness because Jesus stood and declared the authority of the Word of God. It is no coincidence that these things took place after His confrontation with the devil. Jesus first established Himself in His place of authority by overcoming temptation by declaring the Word of God. It was then that He was empowered to "turn the light on" for the people. His life became an eternal blessing everywhere He went.

He preached the Word. After establishing His authority in the Word, the first thing Jesus did as the pattern Son was to preach the Good News of the gospel to the people. His first message was, "Repent, for the kingdom of heaven is near" (Matt. 4:17, NIV). And when He preached to them, they were able to hear the Word because of the anointing of the Holy Spirit that was upon Him. The people testified that no man had ever spoken as He did. He did not teach as the scribes did—but with authority (Matt. 7:29). I believe that because Jesus had defeated the devil in the wilderness, the devil could no longer deceive the people by hindering them from hearing the Word of God.

Many times Christians attempt to do evangelistic and missions' work without having first found the place of true authority and standing in it according to the Word of God. Without doing that, we cannot dismiss the devil who continually comes against us (using his lesser imps, of course).

He keeps us so busy fighting the "forces of the enemy," focusing our attention on his lying strategies, that we simply can't be released into what Jesus has called us to do. We need to focus our attention on Jesus and the authority that comes to us through His life once again.

He called His disciples. As Jesus went about preaching the Good News, He began to call His disciples. I believe that through that same authority His disciples were released to respond to His call to follow Him. Of course, they were the ones that God had ordained should be His disciples. But there was a divine dynamic involved that compelled them to leave their lifestyles in a moment to follow this fascinating preacher.

As I studied what Jesus did, I thought how strange it would be if one of us would go into a store in our local community and just say to the clerk there, "Follow me." I don't think we could expect the same response that Jesus received from those who became His disciples. Why could Jesus do that? Because He had stood in His authority. The enemy was no longer able to blind the people to the truth of God's dwelling in Jesus—the light could shine through. He was released to the divine purposes of God, which included making disciples of these men.

He healed the multitudes. The Bible teaches that "God anointed Jesus of Nazareth with the Holy Ghost and with power: who went about doing good, and healing all that were oppressed of the devil; for God was with him" (Acts 10:38). Jesus not only began to preach and teach and call His disciples, but He went about healing all manner of sickness and all manner of disease among the people through the anointing of the Holy Spirit. The Scriptures teach that great multitudes followed Him—not just a few people, but great crowds.

It is time that Christians discard the mentality of reaching one or two people here and there occasionally for Christ. We need to expect that the *multitudes* will start hearing the truth of the Word of God. Jesus died for the whole world, and He is not willing that any should perish (2 Pet. 3:9). As we establish our authority on the Word of God and allow our desires to become one with God's, our compassions will be enlarged to reach the multitudes.

OUR AUTHORITY ESTABLISHED

PASTOR LARRY LEA, who has been a national leader of prayer for many years, tells how he came face to face with principality sent from the enemy to prevent his new church from flourishing in Rockwall, Texas. When his church began to pray for the powers of the enemy over their area to be bound and for God's light to break through on the people, their prayers stirred satanic resistance to their godly desires.

One day while Larry was standing in his sanctuary praying, the enemy came to resist him. Pastor Lea said that he felt the presence of the enemy to such a degree that it was terrifying. The being that he saw in his spiritual vision stood before him holding a large silver chain in his hands. The enemy threw this challenge at him: "Do you really mean it? Are you serious? Are you going to take your stand?"

Larry Lea realized that he was face to face with the very power that was holding back the harvest of souls that God wanted to bring to their church. It was this evil power, this strong man, that was binding the people in their community from seeing the light. "Immediately," Larry Lea said, "that inner man within me stood up. Before I knew what I was doing, I literally stood to my feet and shouted back at this being, 'You are mighty right! I do mean what I'm saying! I am taking my stand.'" With that cry, Larry Lea stepped toward the shadowy being and saw it slink backward. He knew he had him on the run. The last thing he saw in his vision was this cowardly spirit being drop his chain and disappear. Within one year after that encounter, thirty-four hundred souls had come to Christ and had become a part of Pastor Lea's church.[1]

There is nothing else that Jesus can do for us to establish

our authority in God—His work is complete. We must determine not to be denied the promises that are ours. We must understand that by simply taking our stand on the Word of God we will displace the usurper king—the devil— and all his destructive purposes. The church is going to do a fantastic work in the days ahead. We are going to realize that, after all, we are fighting a spiritual battle and that we're going to win it in the spiritual realms by using the authority we have been given by Christ. The enemy has kept us from doing this through deception, making us think that he is a very strong foe whom we should fear. We need to recognize him for the liar that he is and place our confidence in the written Word of God that has always defeated him.

Even in our most difficult and trying situations we can know the same triumph that Jesus did over His flesh when He agonized in Gethsemane, surrendering to the will of the Father. Did the devil win in that terrible place? Never! It was there that the eternal battle was won—taking our Lord all the way to Calvary.

FOUR

THE PATTERN SON: FROM GETHSEMANE TO CALVARY

IN GETHSEMANE, Jesus overcame the enemy through His obedient surrender to the Father's will. In that lonely place where our Lord struggled against evil to the point of sweating great drops of blood, He bought our obedience for us. By faith we can expect to fulfill all obedience as we allow Christ to walk that obedience out through our lives again.

Incarnate obedience is the greatest power on earth. The life that is fully surrendered to obedience becomes a living sacrifice, and sacrifice of self releases great spiritual power. Jesus, the Son of God, "became obedient unto death, even the death of the cross" (Phil. 2:8). The Father accepted Jesus' supreme sacrifice as the price to deliver us from the penalty and power of sin. Jesus laid down His life willingly to redeem us from the curse of sin, becoming sin Himself. That ultimate sacrifice gave all mankind the authority we need to overcome evil.

In contrast to obedience that results in life, rebellion against God is the power of the demonic—a driving, destructive force that brings only death in every dimension. Disobedience allows death and destruction to reign in our lives and even in our churches. The antidote to the effects of every demonic force is utter abandonment to the will of God.

The Cross—"It Is Finished"

In most religious movies that portray Jesus' Crucifixion, we see Him become weaker and weaker while He is hanging on the cross until finally, in a tortured whisper, He says, "It is finished" (John 19:30). Then He hangs His head to die. That is not the way the Bible depicts this terrible scene. Three of the Gospels declare that Jesus *shouted* with a loud voice from the cross to the very end (Matt. 27:50; Mark 15:37; Luke 23:46). It was not in a whisper of defeat, but as a declaration of triumph that Jesus cried out, "It is finished."

Jesus did not mean "I am finished" when He uttered those words and died. He wasn't referring to what seemed to everyone there like ultimate defeat in His death on the cross. His triumphant declaration, "It is finished," rattled everything around Him—the ground shook, the light fled the sky, graves opened, and saints walked around. There was no small stir in the city! Why? Because through His supreme obedience Jesus was declaring that He had finished the work He had been given to do from before the foundation of the world.

In eternity past where the plan of Redemption was conceived in the Godhead, the Word chose to become the Son (John 1:1). As the only begotten Son of the Father, He knew that this moment of agonizing triumph awaited Him in a tragic moment of time.

When Jesus declared that His work was finished, in essence He was declaring that no one could add anything to it, no one could improve upon it, and nothing else would have to be done to effect our redemption. He had spoiled principalities and powers and had made an open show of them—He had completed the eternal plan of Redemption established in the Godhead before time began.

Finished, in the Greek, is the word *tetelestai,* which means "to accomplish, to complete, to fulfill a destiny." It does not indicate merely an end of something, but of bringing it to perfection, to a destined goal. In the wilderness, Jesus declared His authority based on the Word of God, not based upon His feelings, not based upon the "electricity" of the anointing, but based upon God's Word.

In the agony of Gethsemane, He fulfilled all obedience, surrendering to the cup the Father required Him to drink. But His work was not finished until He had suffered those agonizing hours on the cross, enduring the pangs of physical death. In those last moments, Jesus knew that He had completed His destined goal to perfection. When Jesus cried out, "It is finished," He was declaring, "I have perfectly fulfilled the goal of My destiny. I have been able to accomplish everything I was sent here to do." He knew that all authority was His as He gave Himself in ultimate sacrifice for the redemption of mankind, fulfilling the eternal plan of salvation in every detail.

Peter understood this reality of Christ's finished work when he declared, "Who [Jesus] is gone into heaven, and is on the right hand of God; angels and authorities and powers being made subject unto him" (1 Pet. 3:22). The ultimate victory over sin and evil has been won in Christ's death and Resurrection, completed to the last detail. The Scriptures declare of Jesus that, "having disarmed the powers and authorities, he made a public spectacle of them, triumphing over them by the cross" (Col. 2:15, NIV).

The prophet Isaiah referred to the devil as Lucifer, the one who caused the nations to tremble (Isa. 14:12). But according to the Scriptures, Jesus has spoiled all that terrible power and authority and has taken it away from Satan. He has made an open show of them—the hosts of heaven and the hosts of hell all know the reality of that victory. That is the reason the demons screamed at Jesus, "Why have you come to torment us before the time?" They all knew who

He was and that He had defeated them.

ENFORCING THE VICTORY OF CALVARY

IT IS BECAUSE of the supreme victory of Calvary that believers can walk in triumph over all the power of the enemy. It is not our task to defeat Satan; Jesus has already done that. It is our task only to *enforce the victory of Calvary* in order to enjoy complete victory over the devil in our lives. That ultimate victory, consummated in the death and Resurrection of Jesus Christ, has made it possible for us to fulfill the commission of Christ. Since this is true, we need to answer the question of why we do not see more power manifested in the lives of many believers today.

The answer is that many Christians do not fully realize the significance of the authority Jesus gained over all principalities and powers for our lives. We understand that He bought our salvation. We know that by faith in His name and the work of Calvary our sins are forgiven and we will spend eternity in heaven. But that is not the *completion* of what Jesus bought for us when He cried triumphantly on the cross, "It is finished." His intention was for us to fulfill the destiny of mankind that God had purposed before the fall of man, before Satan usurped authority over our lives to wreak havoc and destruction throughout the history of mankind.

What does that divine destiny look like, and how do we regain it? The Bible tells us that through the cross, Jesus won the right to "present you holy and unblameable and unreproveable in his sight" (Col. 1:22). He was enabled to "reconcile all things unto himself" (Col. 1:20) through the work He did at Calvary. The full promise for Redemption was accomplished there because of His complete defeat and stripping away of the powers of Satan. In order to walk in that victory, it is imperative that we understand our position in God and have a correct perspective of the devil. Though Satan is still an enemy, we must see him completely defeated.

We are not called to fight the devil; rather we are commissioned to *enforce the victory of Calvary.* In that victory we see the absolute obedience to which we are called and that unfolds our divine destiny in the earth. Before we discuss more fully what is meant by enforcing the victory of Calvary, we need to understand who our enemy *is,* and, perhaps more importantly, who he is *not.*

FIVE

RECOGNIZING
THE DEVIL'S DEFEAT

E DWARD SILVOSO, in his book *That None Should Perish,* gives a powerful illustration of the plight of many Christians who do not realize their authority in Christ. He tells the experience of General Jonathan Wainwright, who served under General Douglas MacArthur's command during World War II, in charge of Corregidor, Philippines. General MacArthur had ordered his generals not to surrender. "No matter what," he commanded them, "don't surrender." But seeing the great slaughter of human life around him, General Wainwright finally ordered his men who were left to surrender to the enemy; he watched sadly as his remaining troops were sent to prisoner-of-war camps all over Asia. Thousands died while in transit. Wainwright was sent to Mongolia where the Japanese guarded him as a prize. He was the only United States' general they would ever capture. Edward Silvoso describes Wainwright's plight:

> During those terrible years of captivity, Wainwright labored under tremendous guilt. As he saw his body

deteriorate and become dependent on a cane to move around, he also saw his soul experience even greater deterioration. He felt like a total failure for having surrendered Corregidor.[1]

As MacArthur continued to take possession of island after island, the happy day finally came for the whole world when ultimate victory was declared for the Allies. As MacArthur moved his troops into Tokyo, the news spread quickly that Japan had surrendered to the Allies. However, General Wainwright was in Mongolia, a great distance from Tokyo, and the Japanese commandant was able to keep the news from Wainwright for a while. Silvoso writes:

Can you picture the Japanese commandant watching Wainwright *after* Japan's surrender? He knew they would soon switch places, and the commandant must have trembled at the possibility of facing a captive who would become his captor. Every time he saw him, the Japanese commandant must have felt tremendous uneasiness. A fully armed, properly fed commandant, with more than adequate military force at his disposal, was afraid of the weak, emaciated, dysentery-plagued remains of a ragtag army and its limping general. Why? Because the commandant's power over them was based on a lie. I can picture him wondering, *Has he found out the truth yet? If he has, what will happen to me?*

Eventually, an allied airplane landed near the prisoner-of-war camp where General Wainwright was imprisoned. An American officer walked up to the fence, saluted, and announced: "General, Japan has surrendered." Armed with that piece of truth, Wainwright limped all the way to the commandant's office. He opened the door and without even raising his voice, asserted, "My commander in chief has defeated your commander in chief. I am in control now. You must surrender." Without firing a shot, the emaciated, physically handicapped prisoner of war took over the camp from the well-fed, heavily armed commandant.[2]

Silvoso points out that only Wainwright's ignorance of the truth had kept him a prisoner of war longer than he needed to be! What a picture this dramatic incident is of our status with the devil! It is the enemy's job to deceive us and keep us from knowing our authority in Christ, for with that knowledge comes his certain humiliation and defeat.

As we sit in our various forms of captivity, suffering the effects of the enemy's tyranny, he knows that on the day we realize we are the victors, he will become the victim. In this way, the enemy kept me from knowing how to be born again for six years, though I was active in my Methodist church. I was openly seeking salvation, but no one could tell me how to get saved. Finally, I heard a true testimony of salvation that was shared at a Methodist youth retreat, and I was born again that night.

It took me two more years to figure out how to get baptized in the Holy Spirit. It seemed as if a great conspiracy of secrecy surrounded me to keep me from entering into that experience in God. People around me who had received the baptism of the Holy Spirit would whisper in my presence about what God was doing, thinking it would offend me if I knew they spoke in tongues. Finally, an Episcopalian prayer-group leader who had been Spirit-filled learned of my salvation. She called me and told me I could receive a baptism in the Holy Spirit that would empower my life. If only the devil could have kept me from knowing the truth, he could have succeeded in minimizing my influence for God in the building of His kingdom.

In this same way, the enemy would love to keep the truth from us concerning our authority over all the power of the enemy. If he can just keep us in our little "prisoner-of-war camp," daily struggling for survival, he can cause us to miss the reality of our freedom in God. Not only individuals suffer this prisoner-of-war syndrome, but entire churches sometimes resemble prisoner-of-war camps. Some churches have better prisoner-of-war youth training camps and more developed music departments than other churches. But the real fact is that these churches sit in bondage because they have never learned the victory that is theirs in Christ. They are content with their church activities. They have not tried to confront the enemy in order to bring souls into the kingdom. They may not even realize they need to be set free from personal strongholds that keep them powerless victims of sin. They have never understood that the devil has been defeated and that they are now the rightful authorities in the land. Too many charismatic Christians are laboring in futility because of their erroneous theology about the devil.

CHARISMATIC VS. HISTORICAL THEOLOGY OF THE DEVIL

THE CHARISMATIC COMMUNITY is only now beginning to realize that there have been extremes in what has been taught regarding the believer's position in relationship to the devil. Too many Christians have had a "big devil and little God" concept. Others have believed in a big God—but feared a devil who was almost as powerful. They function as those who are still trying to defeat Satan, although they would never state it this way. Misunderstanding Satan's limitations, they have imagined that he is after them all day long. And he loves for them to be deceived in this way.

The approach of many modern-day Christians has been a theology of dualism—God and Satan fighting about who is in charge, with believers as Ping-Pong balls tossed to and fro in the fray. Such an idea keeps us in a place of irresponsibility in our own lives. It is easier to blame the weaknesses of our flesh on the devil than to take responsibility for our own wrong choices. Remember, the devil did not *make* you do it. He can't make you do anything. He can only tempt, deceive, and accuse. He has no power to make you do anything you don't want to do. When we take responsibility for our own choices and actions, we put the devil's power in proper perspective. Then we can manifest God's authority over the devil through our obedience to the life of Christ within us.

Historically, the church taught a doctrine concerning Satan that firmly put him in his place. When we read volumes written in an earlier century such as *The Christian in Full Armor* or *Quiet Talks About the Tempter,* we quickly realize that our generation has had a theology of the devil that makes him far too prominent and, in the end, makes the believer a victim of Satan's whims.[3]

For example, William Gurnall, in *The Christian in Full Armor,* speaks of Satan's limitations—showing us that God has set boundaries on the evil Satan can do. It is not Satan's prerogative to hinder whom he pleases. He writes:

> The devil may not tempt anyone unless God allows it. When Christ was led into the wilderness, He was led, not by an evil spirit, but by the Holy Spirit (Matt. 4:1). All that transpired was by God's permission.[4]

Gurnall writes as well of the Christian's certain victory and of Satan's certain doom:

> Satan with all his wits and wiles will never defeat a soul armed with true grace, nor will the contest ever end in a stalemate. Even though he *seems* to be overmatched by Satan's supernatural manifestations, there are two reasons why the Christian is yet so unconquerable: 1) There is a curse that lies upon Satan (Gen. 3:14–15), and 2) God uses Satan's schemes to accomplish His own purposes so that Satan is continually baffled.[5]

Christians in our generation must gain this perspective of Satan in order to establish our authority in the earth. We must never agree with the prevalent philosophy that we are victims—victims of heredity, poor parenting, society's prejudice, and others. That is what Satan wants us to believe. Through Christ we are more than conquerors over every destructive situation that we have to face. How Satan wishes you would never find this out! Not knowing this truth keeps us from being the victors we were meant to be.

A BIBLICAL PORTRAIT OF THE DEVIL

HAVING DECLARED THAT we are not victims, but victors, and that it remains only for us to learn to stand in our authority to enjoy our great victory over the enemy, we need to ask the question, "What is the true nature of our enemy?"

What do the Scriptures say of him? He is a liar and the father of lies, according to the Scriptures (John 8:44), so we can be sure he will not paint an accurate picture of himself to us. How can we know our true position in relationship to him? If we have been cringing before a cowardly, defeated bully, what is the true perspective we should have of this conquered enemy?

It is true that Satan once had great power before the throne of God. But when iniquity was found in him, and he actually wanted to dethrone God so he could enthrone himself, he was cast out of heaven (Isa. 14:12). The prophet Ezekiel gives us one of the most vivid biblical portraits of this archenemy of God:

> Thou wast perfect in thy ways from the day that thou wast created, till iniquity was found in thee. By the multitude of thy merchandise they have filled the midst of thee with violence, and thou hast sinned: therefore I will cast thee as profane out of the mountain of God: and I will destroy thee, O covering cherub, from the midst of the stones of fire. Thine heart was lifted up because of thy beauty, thou hast corrupted thy wisdom by reason of thy brightness: I will cast thee to the ground, I will lay thee before kings, that they may behold thee.
> —EZEKIEL 28:15–17

He was a beautiful creature according to the prophet,

perfect in all his ways until iniquity was found in him. As his heart was lifted up, his beauty was corrupted. He was called profane and was cast out of the mountain of God. *Profane* means "defiled as a result of breaking one's word, prostituting oneself and wounding another." The enemy's beauty was defiled when he betrayed God with his desire to be exalted above Him. Satan challenged the holy nature of God. Such insurrection and rebellion could not be tolerated in the presence of God, and so Satan was cast down from that holy presence. Do you know who the devil really is? He is an unemployed cherub.

God created a beautiful being, an archangel who gathered up praise and worship before the throne of God. Music was formed in and through him. Lucifer knew all there was to know about worship. That's why he is effective many times in his attempts to get people away from worshiping God in spirit and in truth. His rebellious spirit that "thinks he knows the right way" infects Christians (especially musicians). That spirit sometimes causes movements and churches to split because of disagreements over the emphasis or forms of worship.

Of course, the devil's ultimate desire is to divert worship from God and receive worship unto himself. Causing confusion in the body of Christ regarding the whole issue of worship is simply a tactic he uses to gain his ultimate end. The Scriptures are clear about his wicked desire to "ascend [and] . . . be like the most High" (Isa. 14:14; Ezek. 28:15). It will help us to thwart our enemy's objective if we understand that the devil's primary desire is not to get us to sin. Though he uses sin as a means to his end, what he ultimately desires is to be worshiped himself.

That is why he tried to get Jesus to worship him, declaring, "All these things will I give thee, if thou wilt fall down and worship me" (Matt. 4:9). Though he failed with Jesus, he still tempts men today to worship anything rather than the true God. All sin creates a breach, a separation, in our relationship to God (Isa. 59:2). Our sin that keeps us from worshiping God in purity and holiness aids Satan in his wicked desire to turn men from God and receive worship himself.

What a tragic thought! Satan had been created with a divine position before the throne of the Father. What kind of authority did he once possess that he actually thought he could pervert it to become equal with God? And what position did he enjoy in heaven that would allow him to take a third of the angels into rebellion with him? (See Revelation 12:4.)

Though we cannot imagine such realms of divine authority, we understand that when he perverted his legitimate God-given authority in rebellion against the greater authority of God Himself, he was cast down from heaven and is now doomed for eternity. Though he had great beauty, rare wisdom, and close fellowship with God, he lost it all when he tried to usurp the place of God.

In the Garden of Eden, the devil was still competing with God, trying to get mankind to defy the command of God and to "become as gods" (Gen. 3:5).

He had failed in his own attempt to ascend and dethrone God, but he had not given up his iniquitous thought and way.

Here in Paradise, he was perpetrating his evil on mankind through *temptation, accusation,* and *deception.* He tempted Eve to disobey God and eat of the tree of the knowledge of good and evil. He accused God of lying about the consequences that man would suffer by choosing to disobey the command of God. And ultimately he deceived Eve into sinning against God. Through that deception all mankind was condemned to suffering the consequences of disobedience.

The Good News of the gospel is that through our obedience to Christ as believers we can be delivered from the terrible consequences of sin in this life and for eternity. We are no longer victims of Satan's rebellion perpetrated against mankind.

PRESENT REALITY OF OUR VICTORY

IN THE NEW Testament, it is the apostle Peter who describes our present position of victory over the devil: "Be sober, be vigilant; because your adversary the devil, as a roaring lion, walketh about, seeking whom he may devour: Whom resist steadfast in the faith . . ." (1 Pet. 5:8–9). The devil is to be resisted through our faith in Christ, thereby enforcing the victory Christ won for us on Calvary. We don't have to win the victory—we just need to insist on it in the face of Satan's lies.

The apostle James gives this simple instruction for gaining victory over the devil: "Submit yourselves therefore to God. Resist the devil, and he will flee from you" (James 4:7). Again, obedience to God is the key to walking in victory over this threatening foe. Though the devil may roar as a lion, when we have submitted our lives to God, and continually do so, we are instructed to simply resist him and he will run away in fear.

THE DEVIL'S FINAL JUDGMENT

THOUGH OUR STUDY does not concern us with the future of the devil, it is comforting to observe his ultimate end. After Jesus returns for His bride, He will set up His reign on this earth for a thousand years. During that time, according to the Scriptures, Satan will be bound.

> And I saw an angel come down from heaven, having the key of the bottomless pit and a great chain in his hand. And he laid hold on the dragon, that old serpent, which is the Devil, and Satan, and bound him a thousand years.
> —REVELATION 20:1–2

Satan is going to be bound for a thousand years while the saints rule and reign with Jesus. Then Satan will be loosed for a little season and will take up his work of deceiving the nations:

> And when the thousand years are expired, Satan shall
> be loosed out of his prison, and shall go out to deceive
> the nations which are in the four quarters of the earth,
> Gog and Magog, to gather them together to battle: the
> number of whom is as the sand of the sea.
>
> —REVELATION 20:7–8

The purpose of his being loosed is to expose those who
have a feigned allegiance to Jesus. As unthinkable as it may
seem, some people will demonstrate, when Satan is loosed,
that they *prefer* the reign of the pretender prince to the
Prince of Peace! But after this appointed time, Satan will be
judged and put away forever:

> And the devil that deceived them was cast into the lake
> of fire and brimstone, where the beast and the false
> prophet are, and shall be tormented day and night for
> ever and ever.
>
> —REVELATION 20:10

The Scriptures are clear that the devil has a definite end
of his destructions and torment. Perhaps this fact will
inspire faith in our hearts to believe and understand that he
is even now defeated, headed toward his ultimate fate, and
cannot legitimately contend for our victory in Christ.

ENCOUNTERING THE ENEMY

HAROLD CABALLEROS HAS presented a powerful concept of
three areas of conflict that must be overcome for us to be
established in the authority we have in Christ.[6] Only as we
resist the enemy successfully in these three areas will we be
victorious in our own lives and in bringing souls to Christ.
He calls these areas of confrontation the *power encounter,*
the *truth encounter,* and the *allegiance encounter.* Though
they are not completely unrelated, they represent distinct
areas of conflict in which we must overcome sin through

the authority we have in Christ. All three of these confrontations were successfully decided in Jesus' encounters with temptation and evil in the wilderness, in Gethsemane, and on the cross.

The confrontation that occurs when two spiritual powers collide, as when we are casting out a demon in Jesus' name, can be defined as a *power encounter*. An example of a *truth encounter* is when I hear the truth of God's Word preached and it penetrates a stronghold of disobedience or ignorance in my mind. In that moment, I must choose whether I will yield to the truth or maintain the stronghold it has exposed. And my choice to obey or disobey that truth I have heard represents an *allegiance encounter*. If I choose to obey the Word of God, I align myself with His will. If I do not, my allegiance is to the place of disobedience the Word has exposed.

If we are not able to overcome evil temptations or deceptions, it may be because we have not yet settled our allegiance to the Word of God in the truth encounter. The Pharisees in Jesus' day continually revealed their wrong allegiance when He brought them to a truth encounter. They chose to resist the Truth Incarnate in the Son, revealing their allegiance to their father the devil. Others, such as the Samaritan woman Jesus met at the well, responded correctly to their truth encounter with Jesus and came to salvation. Many people were healed by Jesus because they chose to respond positively in faith when Jesus, the Word made flesh, came to them in truth encounters.

Satan lost his great power in heaven in a truth encounter, exposing a wrong allegiance to himself and his passion to receive worship instead of giving it to God. Satan's wicked desire to dethrone God so he could enthrone himself is the basis of all sin—that independent desire to become God and receive the homage to ourselves that belongs only to God. For that reason, all sin keeps us from having power with God, for, in some way, every sin usurps God's authority and exposes a false allegiance. It is as we determine to love the truth and continually give our allegiance to our Lord that we will begin to walk in true authority over the power of the enemy.

A few simple key statements highlight the strategy of our battle against the devil to prevent him from causing us to feel like powerless victims in our separate prisoner-of-war camps. Understanding the battle from this perspective will inevitably guarantee us victory over him. So dramatic are the changes in the lives of people who understand these keys to their authority in God that I have called them *breakthrough concepts*.

Six

Breakthrough Keys

Dick Eastman has written a book called *The Jericho Hour* that challenges us to win every home in the world for Christ. A pygmy in Africa read his book and became inspired to evangelize his heathen community of people who live in trees—not in tree houses—in trees. This pygmy believer called his mission "Every Tree for Christ" and vowed not to stop until he had reached the last tree.

When Eastman found out about the pygmy's efforts and heard that twenty-five hundred pygmies had come to Christ and had built their own Christian village, he traveled by single-engine plane and canoe to their territory by the Ebola River. There he discovered that out of a population of six thousand pygmies, this man had won, not twenty-five hundred, but four thousand to Christ! By simply believing and obeying the biblical principles in Eastman's book, this man had exercised his authority over the power of the enemy and become tremendously fruitful in the kingdom of God.[1] Testimonies like these should inspire us to do the same as we choose to believe the Word of God, renounce the lies of the enemy, and fight the fight of faith.

THE FIGHT OF FAITH

THE ONLY BATTLE we have been called to fight is the "good fight of faith" (1 Tim. 6:12). That is why it is so vital to come to a place of faith in the finished work of Christ and all that it means for our lives. Paul spoke of this fight of faith in his letter to the Corinthians:

> For though we walk in the flesh, we do not war after the flesh: (for the weapons of our warfare are not carnal, but mighty through God to the pulling down of strongholds;) casting down imaginations, and every high thing that exalteth itself against the knowledge of God, and bringing into captivity every thought to the obedience of Christ.
> —2 CORINTHIANS 10:3–5

According to the apostle Paul, there are two kinds of spiritual forces we must contend with in our warfare: *powers* and *strongholds*. He speaks to the Ephesians of wrestling against "powers, against the rulers of the darkness of this world, against spiritual wickedness in high places" (Eph. 6:12). The Living Bible calls these rulers "persons without bodies." The powers are divided into categories in the Scripture. There are several lists in Scripture that name them. The apostle Paul refers to principalities and powers (Eph. 6:12; Col. 1:16). He also adds the terms "rulers of the darkness of this world" and "spiritual wickedness in high places" (Eph. 6:12). So *powers* are those forces outside ourselves that war against the kingdom of God—invisible spirit beings.

Strongholds are forces of darkness within ourselves. The apostle Paul calls these strongholds "imaginations, and every high thing that exalteth itself against the knowledge of God" (2 Cor. 10:5). They are structures of thinking and conduct—mind-sets, mentalities, traditions, strong opinions, and desires to which we are obligated in our mental and emotional responses. These strongholds always oppose the will of God.

We have been given authority over *all* the power of the enemy, including evil spirit forces without and wicked strongholds within our own minds. What many Christians *have not known* is how to release the authority we have by faith so as to be victorious over the wicked powers and strongholds that try to defeat us.

UNDERSTANDING THE BATTLE

IN AMERICAN CHURCHES, we have too often subscribed to a theology of powerlessness, prayerlessness, and unbelief that has resulted in disobedience to the Great Commission. This sad reality has resulted in a lack of fruitfulness in our lives. Living in a culture that places so much emphasis on recreation, we need to understand that life is a battleground, not a playground. No soldier goes to the place of battle and signs up to fight for an hour, a day, or even a week. He understands that his involvement in battle will be a *lifestyle* until the victory is won.

Our first battle is to confront the strongholds in our own minds that have kept us from believing the truth and obeying Jesus' command to go into all the world and make disciples of every man. To do that, we must begin to live in the reality, as we have discussed, that the battle is already won and that we are only called to enforce the victory of Calvary.

As Christians, we must develop a mentality that will not give in to the evil one, being willing to resist him until we have the victory we are seeking. When we are praying for souls, we must not give up until we are winning souls to the kingdom. When we are praying for deliverance from sin, we must not yield until we are free from it.

To persevere in this kind of faith until we are walking in

our God-given authority over all the strategies of the enemy, we need to understand a few simple truths that are keys to unlock our prisoner-of-war cells and set captives free. These keys are basic to true Christianity and can become breakthrough concepts for our lives.

KEY #1—SATAN HAS NO LEGITIMATE POWER OF HIS OWN.

As startling as this statement may seem, it is nevertheless very true. The first key on which we must establish our authority is that *Satan has no legitimate power of his own.* We must learn to stand in the truth of our authority in Christ and understand that the enemy is a defeated foe. According to the Scriptures, Christ has disarmed Satan of all his power and authority:

> Blotting out the handwriting of ordinances that was against us, which was contrary to us, and took it out of the way, nailing it to his cross; and having spoiled principalities and powers, he made a shew of them openly, triumphing over them in it.
>
> —COLOSSIANS 2:14–15

Not only did Christ *disarm* Satan, spoiling principalities and powers in open triumph, He also purposed to *destroy* him:

> Forasmuch then as the children are partakers of flesh and blood, he also himself likewise took part of the same; that through death he might destroy him that had the power of death, that is, the devil.
>
> —HEBREWS 2:14

The Scriptures teach as well that Christ came to destroy the *works* of the devil:

> He that committeth sin is of the devil; for the devil sinneth from the beginning. For this purpose the Son of

God was manifested, that he might destroy the works of the devil.

> —1 JOHN 3:8

The risen Christ Himself declared His position as conqueror when He appeared to John in the Revelation:

> I am he that liveth, and was dead; and, behold, I am alive for evermore, amen; and have the keys of hell and of death.
>
> —REVELATION 1:18

Having the keys of hell and of death demonstrates the reality that Christ has taken all of Satan's authority from him and destroyed his power. If that were not true, Calvary would have been a place of defeat. Instead, Calvary was the ultimate victory that brought complete redemption to mankind from the ravages of sin and of evil.

KEY #2—MAN HAS BEEN GIVEN THE AUTHORITY TO OVERCOME EVIL.

The second breakthrough concept we must grasp is that Jesus has given believers authority to overcome evil:

> I have given you authority to trample on snakes and scorpions and to overcome all the power of the enemy; nothing will harm you.
>
> —LUKE 10:19, NIV

When I cooperate with the devil—"give place" to him—I enthrone him in my life (Eph. 4:27). The Scriptures give a clear picture of this dynamic when Paul tells the Roman Christians:

> Know ye not, that to whom ye yield yourselves servants to obey, his servants ye are to whom ye obey; whether

of sin unto death, or of obedience unto righteousness?
—Romans 6:16

Every time I lie or cheat or give myself to lustful thoughts, I am strengthening the dominion of Satan in and through my life. In the same way, I can enthrone Christ by obeying His Word and His will. I make the decisions continually concerning whom I will enthrone in my life. It is the power of Christ's life in me that enables me to choose correctly and carry out the obedience of Christ in my life.

What would happen if we read these wonderful verses expecting them to work for us just the way they declare they will? What if we exchanged our powerless theology for the truth of the Word of God? If we allow the Word of God to bring us to a truth encounter and choose to give it the allegiance it deserves, we will see the strongholds of unbelief crumble in our minds, and we will begin to experience the reality of these wonderful promises. If we use the authority of the Scriptures that Jesus gave to us, we will enthrone the will of God. If we do not, we enthrone the purpose of the enemy by default alone.

Key #3—Exercising our power of choice establishes us in our authority.

The church has been paralyzed by not understanding the power we exercise daily in our choices. Though the world has enthroned the right of man to choose, the church has abdicated her true authority by not choosing to obey the Word. The power that determines the outcome of the battle in every case is man's power of choice, not the power the devil has. We have seen that the devil has no legitimate power of his own.

Then where does he get his power? He usurps his power from man's wrong choices. When man does not choose to believe the truth and fight the fight of faith, he relinquishes his power to the devil. It would do us all good to post this

Breakthrough Keys

statement in a prominent place where we could read it daily:

The only power Satan has is what he siphons out of our authority. The truth is that Christ has given all authority over the power of the devil to us; therefore, the devil must wait for us to default our position of victory in order to exercise any oppressive, destructive, power against us. This is why the enemy has promoted man's enshrining of his right to choose. Free choice, independent choice, is Satan's hope. That is why every wrong lifestyle has its "rights," and it is considered hatred to challenge those rights to disobey the commands of God. The people demanding such "rights" worship their privilege of choice. Through man's wrong choices the devil reigns, not because he has any power of his own, but because man has abdicated his authority to the evil one.

The enemy knows that the power lies in the element of choice. If he can keep our choices under our own jurisdiction and not submitted to God, he can keep himself in power by working through our wrong choices. God gave Adam and his wife the freedom to choose the tree of life or the tree of the knowledge of good and evil (not just evil). He clearly stated the consequences of choosing the wrong tree. Yet they were seduced by Satan to choose the tree of the knowledge of good and evil. When they did so, they lost access to the tree of life. Their wrong choice caused death—separation from God—and gave Satan the power to dominate their minds and entire lives.

Adam and Eve transgressed the command of God by a decision of their wills—exercising their power of choice. As believers who have accepted Christ's sacrifice for our sins, having been restored to relationship with God, we must still choose every hour of every day not to transgress the law of God. Every time we are confronted with a choice, and we choose to yield to the will of God, we establish the kingdom of God in our lives.

Choosing to obey the will of God over our own carnal, selfish desires establishes us in our authority over the enemy.

Choosing to forgive another's offense, or choosing against anger and retaliation in a difficult situation, will establish the life and love of God within us and break the destructive power of the enemy over our lives. If we yield, rather, to the sin of unforgiveness or anger, for example, the Scriptures teach that we are establishing Satan's kingdom, which results in death:

> Then when lust hath conceived, it bringeth forth sin: and sin, when it is finished, bringeth forth death.
> —JAMES 1:15

Just as our prayers accrue righteousness and are placed in vials in heaven (Rev. 5:8), it is evident that the power of sin accrues destruction over our lives and our nation. Everything we think or do has spiritual consequences for or against God's kingdom. That is why spiritual warfare must become a lifestyle, not a series of battles. We must learn to walk in our authority by continually making right choices and fighting the fight of faith.

LET IT BE DECLARED: SATAN IS A DEFEATED FOE

FOR CLARITY, LET me restate that the basic issue determining our victory over evil is the authority issue rather than an issue of power. Authority has been the issue from the very beginning when Satan rebelled in the very presence of God. His real challenge was, "Who's in charge here?" That is still the issue in spiritual warfare, though it is a settled one if we rightly understand and appropriate the victory of Calvary. As we choose to walk in the victory Christ won for us, we will release the authority He gave us to expose Satan as a defeated foe.

The significance of the promise of Redemption in Genesis 3:15 is that Jesus would crush the head—the symbol of authority—of Satan. Jesus suffered His agonizing death on Calvary in order to restore the headship to mankind that the enemy had taken from Adam. Adam gave up his headship by default through disobedience. And so he lost the dominion that God had given him as well as His relationship with God.

But the Scriptures declare Jesus Christ to be the last Adam—not the second one—*the last one* (1 Cor. 15:45). As the last Adam, Christ regained the dominion that man lost in the fall. So when the Scriptures declare, "I am in Christ and Christ is in me," it means that everything that Christ has gained for me, He will then release through me. (See Romans 8:1; Colossians 1:27.) Because He has defeated Satan, I have defeated him.

Though it is true that Satan is an enemy, it is equally true that he is a conquered enemy. We have been given authority over him. That authority, when exercised over the enemy's power, paralyzes his ability to operate in his power. What Satan does have is long experience in the presence of God, and he knows how the power of God works. But he doesn't have power unless he siphons it out of our authority. This is why he resorts to his "wiles" or plan of attack of deception, temptation, and accusation. He is a liar, a deceiver, and a seducer, because his only hope to be able to rule us is to get us to believe that which is not true.

If we do not exercise our authority in faith, the devil will act as a usurper to exercise authority he does not have, deceiving and gaining victories he has no legitimate right to have. Our great need is to learn by faith to release the authority we have been given to enforce the victory already won for us. Only as we grasp the great truth that Satan is a defeated foe will we be delivered from the "works" mentality of being a Christian. It is not our human efforts that give us victory, but our faith in the work of Christ who defeated Satan. Believe these simple keys:

- Satan has no legitimate power of his own;
- Man has been given the authority; and
- Exercising our power of choice establishes us in our authority.

If you do believe them, these three keys will give us a breakthrough into a realm of faith that guarantees victory over the plan of the enemy. He can no longer feign our defeat through his deceptions.

SEVEN

OUR WEAPONS:
DEFENSIVE AND OFFENSIVE

WHILE IT IS true that we do not have to defeat the devil, the Scriptures teach what seems to be a paradox, that we have been given *weapons* and *armor* to engage in a *battle*. The concepts of weapons and armor are necessarily spiritual concepts, for our battle is a spiritual one.

Only as we fully grasp these concepts can we stand in the authority we have been given, much as occupation troops do in war, to gain the territory Christ won for us. If we do not come to this understanding, we could get entangled in the fray, come out with our faith battered, and never enjoy the victory Christ has won for us.

The armor and weapons the Scriptures describe for us are necessary to enforce the victory of Calvary that has been won for us. America would not sit idly by as another nation pushed back our borders and reclaimed the land for itself. Likewise, the Christian must not allow Satan to reclaim territory that Christ won for us at Calvary. From the place of faith that declares the battle already won, we can march into the enemy's camp and declare that we are in charge.

Enforcing the Victory of Calvary

Nay, in all these things we are more than conquerors
through him that loved us.

—Romans 8:37

A conqueror has fought and won a battle, gaining the territory that was under dispute. One who is more than a
conqueror is one who is standing with authority in that victory that has been won. That is why the apostle Paul
exhorted: " . . . having done all, to stand. Stand therefore . . . " (Eph. 6:13–14). We are to stand clothed in our
armor and wielding our divine weapons. Occupation troops
are sent in to be the present authority for one who has conquered. They almost never have to fire a shot because they
are the acknowledged victors; the war is over.

In order to be fully equipped to enforce the victory of
Calvary and enjoy all the blessings He has bought for us,
the Scriptures declare that a defensive armor has been pro-
vided for us, as well as offensive weapons. The armor Paul
describes for our protection includes the shield of faith, the
helmet of salvation, the breastplate of righteousness, the
gospel of peace, loins girded with truth, and all prayer
(Eph. 6). While we will not discuss each of these in detail
here, we need to be aware that each is vital to our success
in this spiritual battle. If we are experiencing defeat in a situation, it would be good to scrutinize our armor and be
sure we are clothed with faith, salvation, righteousness,
peace, truth, and prayer.

As we see more clearly the basis for our authority, we
understand that though the battle has been won and the
devil is a defeated foe, we must learn to stand in our complete armor in order to enjoy our victory over the devil. Only
in that way can we continually enjoy the freedom and victory
of kingdom living. Because the armor is for our protection, a
provision for our defense against the enemy, it is vital that
we not be missing any part of it. That requires a life of

holiness: living in the Word, loving the truth, walking in right-eousness, and continually giving ourselves to prayer. Only in this way will we be equipped to stand in victory against temptations, accusations, and deceptions of the devil.

While describing faith as the shield in our defensive armor, Paul also characterizes our entire battle as a fight of faith, instructing Timothy to "fight the good fight of faith" (1 Tim. 6:12). In that way, Paul exhorts believers, we will lay hold on eternal life to which we were called. That statement defines the "fight of faith." It is believing in the finished work of our conquering Lord and laying hold of God's quality of life—eternal life—that has been bought for us.

Too many Christians view eternal life as that unknown existence we will enjoy in heaven after our death. Jesus clearly defined eternal life in His high priestly prayer: "And this is life eternal, that they might know thee the only true God, and Jesus Christ, whom thou hast sent" (John 17:3). Knowing God is more than simply knowing about Him. To know God means to experience His life and to know life as He intended us to know it—free from sin and all oppression and the destructive plans of the devil. Eternal life means relationship with God, fellowshiping with Him, experiencing His provision, and becoming a part of His purposes in the earth. It means freedom from strongholds and every power of darkness. To that end, we must learn to fight the good fight of faith—to enforce the victory of Calvary in our lives.

In the temptation of Jesus, the pattern Son, we saw that the enemy is defeated through our faith in the Word of God. Declaring the Word of God, Jesus defeated Satan in His wilderness temptation. As believers, we must also declare our faith in the Word in order to possess our rightful victory over the enemy. John, the beloved apostle, declared: "For whatsoever is born of God overcometh the world: and this is the victory that overcometh the world, even our faith" (1 John 5:4). It may sound too simple, but until the Word of God prevails in our hearts, bringing us to a reality of faith, we will not walk in the authority He has given us to enjoy victory over the enemy. For that reason, the Scriptures themselves teach us to meditate on the Word of God day and night so that we can have good success (Josh. 1:8).

It is our faith in the Word that will grasp the reality of the victory that has been won for us and will establish us securely in our authority over the enemy. Expressing our faith in the Word as Jesus did in the wilderness will always expose the enemy for the defeated foe that he is. Crying, "It is written" will silence the devil's accusations and dispel his deceptions. As we gird our loins with the truth, we will not be inflicted with the fiery darts of his temptations.

To establish ourselves in faith, we must learn to use the Word of God effectively as a weapon. The Scriptures declare that the Word of God is "sharper than any double-edged sword, it penetrates even to dividing soul and spirit, joints and marrow; it judges the thoughts and attitudes of the heart" (Heb. 4:12, NIV). No force of darkness can stand when the Word of God is wielded against it in faith. That is why it is so vital to live in the Word, meditating on it day and night, and allowing the Holy Spirit to reveal it to us. It is the truth of God's Word that sets us free.

THE WEAPONS OF PRAISE AND WORSHIP

AFTER THE DECLARATION of the Word in faith, two of our most powerful offensive weapons against the enemy are praise and worship. Battles were won in the Old Testament simply by singing praises to God. Paul and Silas caused an earthquake as they sat in prison singing praises at midnight. Though there has been much emphasis on praise and worship during the last twenty years, we still have not tapped the potential of their power to enforce the victory of Calvary. As we learn more perfectly to unite our hearts in praise and worship of the true God, we are going to see the kingdoms of the enemy topple.

Perhaps it is a direct result of Satan's attempt to be worshiped and to dethrone God, perverting the idea of worship, that makes our praise and worship of God the powerful weapon against the enemy that it is. The Scriptures teach that great victory is to be gained through worshiping God. The psalmist had this revelation when he cried:

> Let the high praises of God be in their mouth, and a two-edged sword in their hand; to execute vengeance upon the heathen, and punishments upon the people; to bind their kings with chains, and their nobles with fetters of iron; to execute upon them the judgment written: this honour hath all his saints. Praise ye the LORD.
> —PSALM 149:6–9

What a striking picture of warfare the psalmist paints as he sees the power and authority men have through praise to execute judgment on their enemies. Of course, we must always remember that our enemies are not people, though people may sometimes seem to be the source of our problems. Our battle is a spiritual one, and our enemies are evil forces that would bind us with fetters of fear, anger, unforgiveness, lust, and other manifestations of sin.

A RIGHT HEART ATTITUDE

OUR HEART-ATTITUDE of praise and worship to God is vital in this spiritual battle. If we try to execute vengeance and come against the power of the enemy in a warring spirit in our own strength, we will likely experience anger that is simply a carnal manifestation of our self-life. But when we praise and worship, we loose the power of God. Instead of wasting our time yelling at the devil, we are praising and worshiping God who is going to execute the vengeance needed. "Vengeance is mine; I will repay, saith the Lord" (Rom. 12:19).

In this faith-filled atmosphere of praise and worship, strongholds in our own hearts and minds come down. I teach my congregation that when they are dancing before the Lord and worshiping God, bowing in His presence, they are bringing down the strongholds of the enemy. We are worshiping the Captain of the Lord's Host, and He is taking care of everything that needs to be done for us to enjoy ultimate victory in the battle.

We have seen that Satan desires to have the worship that belongs to God. Satan is far more interested in *worship* than in *sin*. He is more likely to be found in church than in the worst den of iniquity. This fallen angel would rather pervert a person's worship than corrupt his morals, for he knows that perverting our worship will ultimately lead to the corruption of our morals. He understands that the vital issue of life is the motivation of the heart—and he strives to fascinate us with anything other than God Himself. Though our fascination may be with a person, job, a legitimate pastime, or even ministry, none of which are intrinsically wrong of themselves, if that fascination ultimately diverts our worship from the living God, the enemy has triumphed. Though we may not be overtly worshiping him, the enemy gloats in diverting our worship to anything other than God Himself. Satan is after our worship because he is jealous of our worship of God.

WORSHIP IS INHERENT TO MAN'S NATURE

MANY TIMES WHEN believers speak of learning to worship they are referring to ways they have learned to express worship—through music, lifting of hands, or dancing before the Lord. These expressions are only true worship, however, if they reflect the attitude of a heart that is bowing before the Lord. True worship is the humble, obedient condition of our heart toward God. This heart reality is so important because the power of worship is based in our right relationship with God. We express the integrity of our relationship with God through our worship. For that reason the Scriptures declare, "The hour cometh, and now is, when the true worshipers shall worship the Father in spirit and in truth: for the Father seeketh such to worship him" (John 4:23).

It is inherent in our nature to worship. Worship is truly expressed in what you adore, admire, find fascinating, long for, pursue, spend time with by choice, indulge in, seek after, love, appreciate, talk about, dream about, and set yourself to do or get. We are very dedicated to what we worship. We will sacrifice for it. We will give up important things, often everything, for that object of worship. Unfortunately, what many people worship is something less than God Himself. It might not be a heathen idol, but it is a god by definition, nonetheless. Our "god" is that which is most highly esteemed and worshiped. Many who profess to be Christians can be found to be worshiping at the "altar" of their job, family, favorite sport, recreation, money—and the list goes on.

THE ALTARS IN OUR HEARTS

PRAISE AND WORSHIP ARE mentioned four hundred fifty times in the Bible. They are the power weapons God gave to His people, Israel. When the Israelites became idolatrous, God did not ask them to bind or cast out the gods of the land. He asked them to destroy the altars that were built to them:

> Take heed to thyself, lest thou make a covenant with the inhabitants of the land whither thou goest, lest it be for a snare in the midst of thee: but ye shall destroy their altars, break their images, and cut down their groves: for thou shalt worship no other god: for the LORD, whose name is Jealous, is a jealous God.
> —EXODUS 34:12–14

Remember, God isn't asking us to go out to do direct combat with the devil—Jesus already did that and won. He is asking us to tear down the altars in our own hearts that weaken our authority to enforce the victory of Calvary in His name. Those things which absorb our energies—educational pursuits, ambitions, possessions, pleasures, or other "legitimate" time involvements—become altars that must be torn down. It is up to each of us to tear down the altars we discover in ourselves as we embrace the truth of the Word. No one can do it for us.

Christ wants our affections for Himself. It is in the area of our affections, our heart devotion, that Satan continually works to undermine our place of legitimate authority. We must determine to let all the places of worship in our lives be offered to God. As we tear down every other altar we will see our lives established in His authority! Understanding the battle, the armor we have been given, and the weapons we are to wield, we can choose to move from a place of powerlessness to fruitfulness and from defeat to victory.

The two-edged sword of the Word of God becomes a conquering weapon of faith against the lies, accusations, and deceptions of the devil. And our pure worship of God alone enforces His terms of victory over the devil, making us more than conquerors. Walking in these divine provisions, we will be able to bind the strong man and take the spoils of the enemy as Jesus has intended.

EIGHT

BINDING THE STRONG MAN

MANY CHRISTIANS GET excited when they read in the Scriptures about binding the strong man. They think, "Oh, good, if I can just get the devil bound then I can spoil his house."

> If I cast out devils by the Spirit of God, then the kingdom of God is come unto you. Or else how can one enter into a strong man's house, and spoil his goods, except he first bind the strong man? and then he will spoil his house.
>
> —MATTHEW 12:28–29

I don't blame people for trying to bind the devil any way they can. That's a wonderful thought! It's just that there's more involved in binding the strong man than simply saying, "Satan, I bind you." Such declarations can be empty of power and bring only frustration to the sincere Christian who is unaware of our true scriptural basis for victory.

Jesus described the devil as a strong man who is armed,

and because he is, he keeps his goods in peace.

> Now if I drive out demons by Beelzebub, by whom do your followers drive them out? . . . When a strong man, fully armed, guards his own house, his possessions are safe. But when someone stronger attacks and over- powers him, he takes away the armor in which the man trusted and divides up the spoils.
> —Luke 11:19, 21–22, NIV

What are the goods of this armed enemy—this strong man? And what is the armor in which he trusts? The strong man in our lives is the one that prevents us from enjoying the eternal life God wants us to enjoy. He is the one who keeps the souls of men—your precious young person, your husband, your wife, your friend for whom you're praying—in the house of his lies, holding them cap- tive to his wicked destructions. The armor in which he trusts is our ignorance, our lack of faith, or our disobedi- ence—making the wrong choices that keep us from the place of authority that is rightfully ours.

Many times, though not always, sicknesses are caused by the work of the "strong man." Jesus declared of one woman's illness, "Ought not this woman, being a daughter of Abraham, whom Satan hath bound, lo, these eighteen years, be loosed?" (Luke 13:16). Sometimes the devil is keeping people captive to sickness, sometimes to mental ill- ness, addiction, anger, and all kinds of other sin. And because he is armed, he keeps his "goods" in peace.

What we have to do in fighting the good fight of faith, in order to take what is rightfully ours, is to bind the strong man and take his spoils, or his goods. The word *spoils* is an ancient term that was used in war when the conquering army took the valuables from the defeated enemy. The pre- cious goods taken from the enemy were the spoils that belonged to the conquering army. On Calvary Jesus won the ultimate battle with evil. When He cried, "It is finished,"

He meant the battle was won, the strong man bound, and the spoils were His. That reality makes those spoils ours—the rightful property of every believer who will challenge the strong man. What we are now commissioned to do by our Lord is to go in and take the spoils from the enemy in the authority of Jesus' name.

Jesus said, "When an armed strong man keeps his palace, his goods are in peace." The devil has had a lot of goods in peace for a long time. Since 1963 when prayer was taken out of public schools, he has held our children captive—in peace. Since legislation was passed to legalize abortion, he has held our unborn babies captive—in peace—to destroy their innocent lives. Since homosexuality was legalized, he has held those people in that bondage—in peace. Only as Christians become aggravated and agitated will the dreadful evils of our nation be overcome. Christians must begin rising up to say to the strong man, "We have had enough! We are going to march in and take the spoils from the enemy."

Jesus continued, "But when a stronger than he shall come upon him, and overcome him, he taketh from him all his armor wherein he trusted, and divideth his spoils." Who is stronger than Satan? Jesus has disarmed this strong man. Because of His victory, we must disarm him also. We cannot overemphasize the fact that we must not try to do what Jesus has already done. In order to enjoy the spoils of the victory that He has won, we must enforce the victory through faith.

The Scriptures say that Jesus descended into hell and took captivity captive. He has already declared that the enemy is no longer able to keep those who are not willing to be his. Jesus has already won the victory. On the cross of Calvary, the "stronger than he" came upon the enemy and overcame him—disarming once and for all the strong man.

TAKING HIS ARMOR

THE AMERICAN STANDARD version tells us that as long as the

strong man has his armor, "his possessions are undis-turbed." But the stronger one takes away all his armor on which he had relied and then distributes his plunder. The Greek word *panopleia*, used here for *armor*, is used only two times in the New Testament. It is used here to describe the strong man's armor in which he trusts. The second time it is used by the apostle Paul to describe the saint's armor. Desperate men of war have often declared, "It is him or us." As we learn to stand clothed in our divine armor, we disarm the enemy and can plunder him and take the spoils.

Comparing the armor of the saint to the armor of the enemy shows us how we keep the devil from getting an advantage over us to hurt and harm us. The enemy's armor that he trusts in is the hope that we will not choose to stand completely clothed in our armor. Here we see our power of choice as the determining factor to our spoiling the enemy. If we don't choose to wear the breastplate of righteousness, the enemy has access to us and can hold us captive to un-righteousness, sin, or wickedness. If we do not wield the shield of faith, he holds us captive to doubt and unbelief. If our loins are not girt about with truth, he can work destruc-tion and hold us captive to his lies and deception. When we do not choose to live in obedience to the Word of God, we are left to our intellectual reason. And the Bible says that the carnal mind is enmity against God (Rom. 8:7). It will always bring us to certain defeat.

The armor in which the enemy trusts is that we will make decisions according to our carnal minds instead of our faith in the Word of God. He trusts that we will not walk in the gospel of peace, but in confusion and turmoil. When we put on the helmet of salvation and the breastplate of right-eousness, take up the sword of the Spirit and the shield of faith, have our loins girt about with the truth, and our feet shod with the preparation of the gospel of peace, we keep the enemy from being able to attack us and harm us. When we stand in the armor of God, the stronger one has come, and we are able to bind the strong man. Therefore we spoil his lies as well as the confusion and torment with which he tries to hold us and others captive.

This is the authority that Christ died to give us and that takes away the armor in which the devil trusts. When we take his armor, we are establishing ourselves in our rightful place of authority, which brings victory into our lives and situations. The strongholds that are in our minds through imaginations and vain things that exalt themselves against God are brought down through our obedience as we put on the whole armor of God (2 Cor. 10:4–5). Through our obedience, the strong man is bound, the armor in which the enemy trusts is taken away, and we are able to spoil him.

So often the enemy is able to gain an advantage over us because of our wrong thinking. Because of strongholds in our own minds, we are not able to bind the strong man to bring down strongholds that are working in other peoples' minds. Binding the devil is not about repeating over and over, "I bind you—I bind you again—I bind you tighter." The binding of the strong man is not words, it's not noise, it's not gritting your teeth and clinching your knuckles. It is the spiritual reality of taking away the armor in which the enemy trusted by walking in righteousness, lifting up the sword of the Word and the shield of faith, and walking in the peace that God has said is ours. Only in this way can we disarm the enemy.

It is very important that we become aggressive Christians. Though we must always avoid having a warring spirit, yet in the peace of God we must determine to stand against the encroachment of the enemy. We can spoil the enemy through the simple reality of knowing who we are and knowing that we are standing in our full armor to enforce the victory of Calvary. In that way we will strip the enemy of the armor in which he's been trusting.

NINE

MY JOURNEY FROM PERSONAL CRISIS TO AUTHORITY

A S I STUDIED the truths I have been sharing in this book regarding releasing our authority, I found myself in an unexpected process of "heart surgery" because of certain life situations. It was unexpected only because I had not yet seen the biblical pattern by which God brings us to the realization of our authority in Him.

I had cried out in prayer for more power, as did Carlos Annacondia, telling the Lord that I would use it to serve Him in reaping the harvest.

Though my prayer showed a lack of understanding, God had mercy on my ignorance and proceeded to answer my prayer. He simply arranged some circumstances in my life to do it His way.

THE HEART FACTOR

Keep thy heart with all diligence; for out of it are the issues of life.

—PROVERBS 4:23

As I continued to pray earnestly for more power, mistakenly thinking that was what I needed, the Lord spoke to me from the Song of Solomon with an invitation and a promise:

> Come, my beloved, let us go forth into the field; let us lodge in the villages. Let us get up early to the vineyards; let us see if the vine flourish, whether the tender grape appear, and the pomegranates bud forth: there will I give thee my loves.
> —Song of Solomon 7:11–12

My heart responded afresh to this call to the vineyards, though I had already traveled to many nations and established Bible schools in several. The new harvest field that now opened to me was in the city of Kharkov in Ukraine, part of the former Soviet Union. For ten days I preached crusades, traveling with an accompanying team of mostly young adults who were doing mime and singing worship songs in the Russian language. During that short time, we gave three thousand Russian New Testaments to those who came to make commitments to Jesus Christ. I wept at the incredible harvest into which I had stumbled. In obedience, I had gone with Him into the villages, and He showed me the tender-appearing grapes. I rejoiced in seeing, with Him, the first appearing of this early crop. We saw gray-haired women wearing babushkas and wild-haired young people unashamedly respond to the invitations to receive Jesus as their Savior.

On my second trip to Ukraine in the fall of 1993, I was accompanied by a small team. One place in which we ministered was the Institute for Research, which was under the control of the military. From that audience, a man stood up and asked: "Can you tell me how a person who has been a communist all of his life can walk out of that ideology into what you are talking about?" His openness was astounding.

After I answered his question and finished ministering the simple gospel, the leading medical official of that institute stood and said, "Today we have heard about Jesus Christ and have found out that He will come into our hearts. We believe that we have said yes to Him, that we have received Him today, and that He will never leave us."

I was deeply moved by such childlike faith in accepting the Good News of the gospel. I tried to imagine what the response would have been if I were in a large corporation in the United States, invited by the head of the Research Department to present Jesus Christ to his staff. What a joy to see a large number from this Ukraine audience stand to receive Jesus after hearing my message. Their response was typical of the many audiences to whom we ministered, whether in large halls, in schools, or in the women's prison. Three-fourths of the women prisoners came forward weeping, giving their hearts to Jesus, their hardened hearts moved by the realization of the gift of forgiveness to them.

As thrilling as that was, though I did not know it at the moment, there was more to come in the process that would be an answer to my prayer. It was on my second trip to Ukraine that Jesus fulfilled His personal promise to me from the Song of Solomon. He did what I wanted most of all— He showed me His loves. (See Song of Solomon 7:12.) Christ revealed Himself to me in a way that I had not known Him before.

How do you know if a person really loves you? How does he show you? By opening his heart to you and letting you know who he *really* is. He tells you things about him- self that others haven't heard or cared about. He trusts that you will respond to his love with your love. Though I did not know it, I was about to be overwhelmed by a visitation of the Spirit that would reveal Jesus to me as I had never known Him before.

Simply ministering in Ukraine had impacted me as I watched the overwhelming response of people to the gospel. The desperate hunger I saw in people who had not been allowed to hear the gospel for seventy years had a dramatic effect on my life. As I was preparing to minister in a large hall, I wept as I calculated that hundreds of people had already received Jesus in our few days of ministry there. This was truly a harvest field, and we were simply being allowed to put in the sickle.

Though the chill of the October days had arrived, in my hotel room there was no heat because "Big Brother" (the Ukrainian government) does not turn the heat on until a certain date later in the year. The economic and political conditions in which the Ukrainian people live are depressing. There is a scarcity of food, and much of the housing resembles our large-city ghettos. We had been cold all day—the inside of the auditoriums were the same temperature as the outdoors. There was no place to get warm.

As I was lying there under four or five blankets, shivering from the cold, I attempted to find a little warmth by heating my iron and running it across the sheets before I got into bed. Then I put my robe on upside down over my gown to cover me from my feet upwards. The misery of a severe sore throat that closed up at night aggravated my otherwise dreary situation. During the day I recovered enough voice to preach, but at night I suffered loss of sleep from the pain of my inflamed throat.

In a room where the mercury would not have risen above forty-five degrees, I lay with tears streaming down my face. I prayed, "Jesus, I would not do this for anyone but You."

He didn't respond as I might have expected, saying, "I know, daughter, and I appreciate what you are doing so much. Bless your heart, you are so precious to make this great sacrifice for Me."

I said to Him, "Jesus, You know I am doing this only because I love You."

And I heard Him say so tenderly, "I love you, too."

It was then that He began to reveal Himself to me in a way I had never known Him. It seemed that He sang to my heart the verse: "There will I give thee my loves" (Song of Sol. 7:12). He began to let me know Him as the living

Word. Though I had been teaching His Word for twenty-five years and considered myself a serious student of the written Word, I had not known the Lord, the *living Word,* as He was revealing Himself to me in this intimate encounter with Him. He began to speak to me from the Scriptures that reveal Him as the living Word:

> For there are three that bear record in heaven, the Father, the Word, and the Holy Ghost: and these three are one.
>
> —1 John 5:7

In this verse, the apostle John did not use the well-known phrase, "Father, Son, and Holy Ghost." I believe it was because this beloved apostle understood that in the beginning, before the creation of the world, Jesus was not yet made manifest as the Son; He was known as the Word.

> In the beginning was the Word, and the Word was with God, and the Word was God.
>
> —John 1:1

As I lay in my cold hotel room night after night, God revealed His Word, His very Person, to me in a new way, and I began to know Him as the living Word. He showed me so much in the Scriptures that I returned home with ten new sermons. These ten sermons soon expanded into twenty. My congregation saw such a new anointing in my preaching and such change in my person that they wanted to go to Ukraine themselves to experience the reality I had experienced.

The Lord had given me His loves as He had promised, in the villages and the vineyards. Some might say that shivering in that dark land without the comfortable surroundings of my office and library where I usually prepare them was a hard way to get sermons. But the messages carried a fresh anointing and deeper revelation of Christ and had a greater effect on the lives of people than many that I had prepared in my comfortable study.

The Living Word

THE MOST IMPORTANT thing Jesus showed me during that visitation was that He *is* the living Word. I thought I knew that, having ministered the Word for many years. But when He came to me as the living Word, He began to show me by revelation the meaning of the phrase, " . . . the Word was God." I understood then that all the power of the omnipotent God was resident in the living Word, who was God. The living Word is the creative, transforming, living, pulsating, life-changing force of divine love—the Redeemer of everything it touches. How the words of John the Beloved rang in my heart:

> In the beginning was the Word, and the Word was with God, and the Word was God. The same was in the beginning with God. All things were made by him; and without him was not any thing made that was made.
> —JOHN 1:1–3

The Word was with God at the Creation; and the Word was God. Then He was made flesh, manifested as Jesus the Son, and dwelt among us—God Incarnate, walking the earth as the living Word (John 1:14). Now that He has returned in triumph to the Father, "There are three that bear record in heaven, the Father, the Word, and the Holy Ghost: and these three are one" (1 John 5:7).

All these scriptural realities had been a part of my doctrinal understanding. I accepted them as true. But when Jesus visited me there in that cold Ukrainian hotel room, I began to experience, in more than a doctrinal way, the wonderful reality of the living Word who became incarnate and lived on earth as Jesus Christ. As He continued to reveal Himself to me there, Jesus became inexplicably precious to me as

He willingly opened Himself and we communed together there. Have you known the sweetness of a relationship with a friend where trust has been built in such a way that he says to you, "I am going to tell you something about myself that I haven't shared with anyone because I love you, and I trust you, and I want you to know this about me"? Multiply that sweetness a thousand times, and maybe it would be close to how I felt when Jesus came to reveal Himself to me there.

Having carried for some time the crushing burdens that seem peculiar to pastoral ministry, the Lord knew that I needed to touch Him afresh for myself. When He told me He loved me, He touched my brokenness, healing a deep emotional wound in my heart. And He showed me that it was knowing Him as the living Word that would give me the power to do the work He had asked me to do in the nations.

Other scriptures flooded my mind, all carrying a new dimension of revelation. I remembered Jesus saying in His high priestly prayer: "Neither pray I for these alone, but for them also which shall believe on me through their *word*" (John 17:20, emphasis added). His prayer was not only for His disciples who had believed His Word, but for all who would believe the Word that came through them. Jesus reassured my heart that I was not to worry about anything. I was simply to be faithful and obedient to keep preaching the Word, and His Word would do the work He had set before me. When I came home, I began to preach about the living Word and to teach the people how to enter into deeper relationship with the wonderful Person of our Lord, the living Word.

It is the Word of God that accomplishes the will of God in the earth. The work God had in mind for me in Ukraine began to unfold in the days that followed this powerful visitation of His presence. A man approached me, having the mistaken idea that I had written a book on how to produce television programs. He was himself a producer for Ukraine television and an advisor to the president on communications matters. He asked me if I would do a Christian television program for their city, featuring my preaching as well as music and interviews. Even after I corrected his misinformation, telling him that the books I had written were on other subjects, not on television production, he still wanted me to do the program. We have been reaching Kharkov, a city of two million people, through the preached Word with a television broadcast twice a week ever since.

There has been tremendous response to the program. As a result of that television program, we have been given the opportunity to open a medical diagnostic clinic in the city of Kharkov. Medical people in the United States, having been apprised of this opportunity, are giving us their obsolete equipment to use there. Pharmaceutical supplies also have been given for the clinic. The clinic is a place where people come to receive diagnostic services and medical prescriptions—and we can share the gospel with them while they are there. We have been given a wing of the hospital to be used for this clinic as well as for "spiritual" meetings. We can teach there and do whatever evangelistic work we want to do. God has continued to open this harvest field to us, taking us into a broader realm of missions than ever before. Though we had built a Bible school in India and Indonesia and been involved in other missions works, we had not been involved in so dramatic an aspect of the End-Time harvest before.

My cry for more power had brought me to a place of obedience, to a willingness to go to a harvest field even though I was to experience some physical hardship. I did not know that through my small obedience I was to enter into wonderful revelation of the authority of the living Word who wants to do His wonderful work through us.

It will never be by the stamping of our feet, the pounding of the Bible, or the shouting of the promises of the Word that we gain authority over sin and self or the ability to win souls as we desire. Though that authority is already ours, paid for by the precious blood of the Lamb, we can only enjoy it through relationship with Him—believing His Word and obeying it. Out of that relationship will come the understanding of His will for every situation that we face and the power to confront the enemy's lies that would keep us from realizing the purposes of God. As we learn to release the authority we have through relationship with the Son, we will truly begin to reap the harvest.

TEN

RELEASING THE AUTHORITY

Psalm 110 is the most wonderful psalm in the Bible according to G. Campbell Morgan. Certainly it is one of the most revelatory psalms, giving us wonderful insight into what God is releasing His church to do today. The church is entering into fuller revelation of Jesus' Great Commission than it has had in all of church history. In Jesus' commission of His disciples, He declared that we would not only preach the gospel to every creature and baptize those who believed, but we would also cast out devils, take up serpents, and if we drink any deadly thing, it will not hurt us, and we shall lay hands on the sick, and they shall recover (Mark 16:15–18). After commissioning His disciples, Jesus ascended into heaven to be seated at the right hand of God—until His enemies become His footstool.

REAPING THE HARVEST

The LORD said unto my Lord, Sit thou at my right hand, until I make thine enemies thy footstool. The LORD shall send the rod of thy strength out of Zion: rule thou in the midst of thine enemies. Thy people shall be willing in the day of thy power . . .

—PSALM 110:1–3

"THE LORD SAID UNTO MY LORD . . . "

This psalm is a prophetic picture of the victory of Christ over the enemy and the victory of believers as a result of His victory. Who is speaking to whom when the psalmist uses the phrase "the LORD said unto my Lord?" The Hebrew words used here for *Lord* are two different words, revealing that *Yahweh* (LORD) is speaking to *Adonai* (Lord). That is, God the Father is speaking to Jesus. It was the heavenly Father who told Jesus to sit at the Father's right hand.

"SIT THOU AT MY RIGHT HAND . . . "

After the ascension of Jesus, the Scriptures are clear that He was seated at the right hand of the Father. There He ever lives to make intercession for the saints (Heb. 7:25). The apostle Paul declared that God has also "raised us up together, and made us sit together in heavenly places in Christ Jesus" (Eph. 2:6). According to Jesus' commission to His disciples, He has set us above the enemy, giving us authority over all the power of the devil (Luke 10:19). What God has asked us to do in reaping the harvest could be called a "divine setup." He has set us up above the power of the enemy for the purpose of our personal redemption and for bringing the souls of men and women to Christ. The psalmist understood that it was from that vantage point, seated in heavenly places, that we would put our enemies under our feet.

The devil has done his best to find a way to deceive the saints of God into thinking that he has some sort of authority that he does not have so that he can keep us from walking in our authority that Christ has already given us.

But the fact is, the enemy does not have the authority either to keep us from knowing God or from bringing in the harvest, because Jesus, seated at the right hand of the Father in heaven, has been given all authority in heaven and in earth. According to the Scriptures, He has given that authority to believers, and we are seated with Him in heavenly places.

"UNTIL I MAKE THINE ENEMIES THY FOOTSTOOL. THE LORD SHALL SEND THE ROD OF THY STRENGTH OUT OF ZION . . ."

The apostle Paul declared this same message of the reigning Christ when he wrote: "For he must reign, till he hath put all enemies under his feet" (1 Cor. 15:25). No lying, seductive, usurper in God's kingdom will survive the reigning Christ. All enemies—sinful disobedience, sickness, rebellion, death—ultimately will be put under our Lord's feet.

This is a wonderful reality, but the way it will be realized is even more wonderful. How is He going to reign? How will those enemies be put under His feet? The psalmist declared: "The LORD shall send the rod of thy strength out of Zion" (Ps. 110:2). The Lord is going to rule through Zion—His people—His church. The Lord is not going to send the rod of His strength out of a cloud. He is going to reign through believers like you and me. He must reign *in* every believer until all enemies of disobedience and all rebellious strongholds are conquered and He is Lord of all. And He must reign *through* us, by our taking the authority He has given us to subdue His enemies in the world.

"RULE THOU IN THE MIDST OF THINE ENEMIES . . ."

Where do we rule? In the midst of our enemies. We don't have to wait until our enemies go somewhere else or until we are perfected—we are to rule in the very presence of our enemies. We can be joyful and enjoy a feast while they look on. The psalmist declared this in another place when he wrote: "Thou preparest a table before me in the presence of mine enemies" (Ps. 23:5). I have had to feast in the presence of my enemies at times, those who oppose the vision and the work God has given us to do. I am not going to let my enemies keep me from enjoying the blessings of the Lord.

The church has been commanded to rule in the midst of our enemies. They cannot move us from our place of victory. As we enforce the victory of Calvary, they will be displaced, either coming to repentance and joining our celebration, or fleeing before the rod of God.

"Thy people shall be willing in the day of thy power . . ."

Some may say lazily, "Well, I don't know if I feel like being a soul winner." We don't have that option. We have been given a commission to fulfill. As God fills the church anew with His power, willingness will characterize the true believer who understands the authority he has been given. "Thy people shall be willing in the day of thy power."

The church is coming to a place of faith to believe that we have authority over the enemy, and we are excited about that reality and committed to it. Everything that God plans to do in the earth, He does through the people that believe Him. The church is ordained to subdue the enemies of Christ in the earth. As we do, we are going to see multitudes come to the saving knowledge of Christ before the end comes.

The Sign of His Coming

> Tell us, when shall these things be? And what shall be the sign when all these things shall be fulfilled?
> —Mark 13:4

A. B. Simpson was interviewed in the late 1800s by a journalist who asked him, "Do you know when Jesus will return?"

He replied, "Yes, and I will tell you if you write exactly what I say, including references, and nothing more." The journalist agreed. Simpson said, "Write down Matthew 24:14: 'And this gospel of the kingdom shall be preached in all the world for a witness unto all nations; and then shall the end come.'"

The journalist wrote those words and then, looking up expectantly, asked, "What else, sir?"

Simpson replied, "Nothing else."

When the true gospel of the kingdom is preached in all the world, the Scriptures declare, the end will come. That is why we must be committed to reaping the harvest. In his book *The Jericho Hour,* Dick Eastman made a interesting observation: Someone wrote a book titled, *Eighty-eight Reasons Christ Will Return in 1988.* When 1988 had come and gone without the coming of Christ, Bob Hoskins wrote a book titled *UNFINISHED: 2.7 Billion Reasons Christ Didn't Come in 1988.*[1] His title, of course, referred to the people who did not yet know Christ. Christ will return when the gospel is published in all the nations. That fact is also the sign of His coming.

The word *nations* used in Scripture does not just refer to the recognized political entities present in the world today. It should be translated more accurately as *ethnos* groups. The word *ethnos* includes every tribe and language represented on the earth.

In the Book of Revelation, we read, "And they sung a new song, saying, Thou art worthy to take the book, and to open the seals thereof: for thou wast slain, and hast redeemed us to God by thy blood out of every kindred, and tongue, and people, and nation" (Rev. 5:9). It is not enough to have a witness in the recognized nations of the world; the gospel must be preached to each linguistic and people group everywhere. Out of twenty-four thousand people groups in the world, there are still eight thousand left to be reached with the gospel.[2]

There are thousands of Christians in the United States alone who are not yet a part of reaping the harvest. Strongholds of the enemy in our own minds have kept God's people even from looking on the harvest. Why are we so caught up in our own lives and problems, or even our own church-oriented "ministries"? The enemy has used seemingly good pursuits to rob us of the opportunity to rejoice through sowing and reaping in the harvest!

Strongholds, as we have said, are harmful ways of thinking—unbelief, pharisaical attitudes, the bondage of religion, tradition, culture, and prejudice—all such things that form our mind-set out of which we live our lives. Jesus had a mind-set regarding the harvest. He said to His disciples:

> My meat is to do the will of him that sent me, and to finish his work. Say not ye, There are yet four months, and then cometh harvest? Behold, I say unto you, Lift up your eyes, and look on the fields; for they are white already to harvest.
>
> —John 4:34–35

We must agree with the mind-set of Christ and walk in the authority He has given us to reap the harvest we have not yet looked upon. As we allow Christ to rule in us to conquer these strongholds we will begin to reap the harvest.

According to C. Peter Wagner's study, the following are reasons why American Christians have not moved out into reaping the harvest as people have in other nations:

- We are waiting until we are perfect before working in the harvest.
- We regard the "deeper life" experience (holiness) as an end in itself.
- We expect ministry to self-generate from a holy life.
- We relate effectiveness in ministry (success) to outward compliance with certain standards.[3]

We have been laboring in the church under some serious religious misconceptions. Religious mentalities that have kept the church from going out to reap the harvest must be regarded as deceptions of the enemy. Waiting until we are perfectly healed before going with the gospel or making holiness an end in itself are wrong concepts that have formed strongholds in our minds and kept us from reaping the harvest.

Of course, we are to pursue holiness through prayer and worship, but not to the exclusion of telling our neighbor about Christ and sharing the reality of our hope of eternal life. Prayer, as vital a part of our Christian lives as it is, should never be seen as an end in itself. We can be deceived even in our praying, becoming religious and completely ineffective in building the kingdom of God.

An example of living according to religious misconceptions may be seen in the Charismatic movement of Argentina, which has experienced two major revivals in this century. The first revival, occurring during the 1980s, was a healing revival that fostered a mentality that "we must heal the church before we can save the world." Because the people were never satisfied with the extent of the healing work being done in the church during this revival, they did not go out to win souls to the Lord.

The second Argentine revival during the 1990s brought supernatural manifestations along with healing. This time the church went out into the harvest immediately. It is this present move of the Spirit that has brought such phenomenal increase in the church of Argentina.[4] Even when God is moving in revival, it is vital that we focus our hearts and minds correctly to see the purposes of God accomplished.

Wherever our theology or Christian dogma and practice do not reflect the passion and focus of our Lord, we must determine to change that wrong thinking and agree with His Word and His commands. Jesus said He came to seek and to save that which was lost (Luke 19:10). He has sent us into the world even as the Father sent Him into the world (John 20:21). As the church, the body of Christ, we must begin to resemble Him in motivation, desire, and ultimate results in building His kingdom in the earth.

THE HARVEST DECADE

AT THE BEGINNING of this decade men began to awaken to what God is doing in the earth, rather than what they "think" should happen. More recently, the Holy Spirit has begun to pour out a fresh anointing of renewal and refreshing on His people. This latest move of the Holy Spirit has brought joy to the church, a return to our first love, healing of emotions along with an increase in faith to believe God for the harvest. The tremendous increase in the harvest of souls already during this decade is proven by hard statistics. What can we expect to see before the end of this decade, which is also the beginning of a new millennium, as God continues to move in the hearts of His people?

In the late 1800s, A. B. Simpson's burning message was filled with the conviction that only by reaching all peoples with the gospel would Jesus return. That fiery message launched the Christian Missionary Alliance Church, and within six years of their founding, they had one hundred eighty missionaries in twelve different mission fields of the world. Simpson believed that the gospel must be taken to each people group so that a people could be taken out of every nation for God.

In 1885 A. T. Pierson gave the following challenge at Moody's Bible Convention: If ten million of the four hundred million Christians in the world would reach one hundred souls in fifteen years, the whole world would have heard the gospel by the turn of the century—1900! Sadly, in 1895 he stood to acknowledge to the convention that it would not be done.[5] The good news is that complete evangelization of the world would be ten times easier to do today than it was then. Projections were made in 1993 that of the five hundred forty million Christians in the world today, each believer would need to reach only ten unbelievers with the gospel in the next seven years in order to accomplish that goal.[6]

In this decade, our evangelical resources have increased

86

in numbers of missionaries on the field ten times over the number of missionaries in 1895. The Third-World countries alone have raised ten thousand missionaries in the last two years. Our financial base is twenty times greater than that of 1900.[7] In 1900 there were fifteen people born for every one person who was born again. In 1992 for every two people born on earth—one person was born again![8]

A New Millenium

A NEW MILLENIUM is upon us—the year 2000. Many believers are anxiously awaiting what God might be wanting to do at that time. We're not waiting statically or stagnantly—we are waiting *expectantly* and giving ourselves to God's purpose during the interim. Do I state the obvious when I say that we have not changed milleniums for almost a thousand years? Have we considered the significance of that fact? Even the turn of a century historically has often resulted in climactic events in the spiritual realm. Before the turn of the last century, about 1895, people all over the world began receiving the baptism of the Holy Ghost and speaking in tongues.

This newly outpoured Pentecost really began blazing in 1906 at Azusa Street, but people were receiving the baptism of the Holy Ghost several years before that time. There were churches in our area of Tennessee (please excuse me, I do not mean to indulge in cultural pride) that were speaking in tongues in 1895 and 1896. Actually, not very far from where I live, in an area where the Cherokee Indians now reside, people received the Holy Ghost during those early years. Then on New Year's eve of 1899, in a Bible school in Kansas, on the eve of the turn of the century, Charles Parham and his students started speaking in tongues after seeking the baptism of the Holy Spirit. Soon they began to publish the news of this supernatural experience, and it spread like wildfire to many cities.

One hundred years later, we are in that same framework

of time at the turn of another century, only this time we are also changing milleniums. We are a hundred years closer to the return of Jesus, and we have much greater expectancy for the great End-Time harvest to be reaped before He comes back again.

A Threshold Generation

I BELIEVE THIS generation is a threshold generation. There are only three thousand unsaved people groups left to reach. We are the first generation that has radio, television, computers, jumbo jets, communication, transportation, finances—everything that is needed to reap this harvest. And God is doing phenomenal things in many parts of the world through those means.

Albania, a country that is on record as being completely atheistic, has opened three hundred active churches in the last few years. In Nepal, Jesus has appeared to Nepalese people while they were standing in their yards. They saw Him hanging on a cross in the clouds. In their fright, they called the police. The police received hundreds of calls from people who said, "There's a man hanging on a cross in the clouds."[9]

In a mosque in the Middle East, Jesus appeared to nine Muslim holy men, who immediately turned their lives over to Jesus Christ. That has created no small stir in their area. An entire Malagasy village was converted when one insane woman was delivered of demons by a Lutheran pastor. Every person in that village came to Jesus. Within three weeks they had built a church to worship the Christ.[10] These are only a few examples of what is already happening in this "greater-works generation." Worldwide, the church is expanding at a rate of three times the general population.

Luis Bush of the A.D. 2000 and Beyond movement says that the motivational goal of their movement is to reach the remaining unevangelized people by the end of the millenium—December 31, 1999![11]

WORLD-WIDE IMPACT

BECAUSE MANY CHRISTIANS have been involved only in their local church community, they do not realize how powerful the work of the Holy Spirit has already been in our century. Since the Holy Spirit was poured out at the turn of this century, the Pentecostal movement has continued to multiply at phenomenal rates. In 1945 the Pentecostal movement numbered sixteen million. By 1965, during the Charismatic renewal, it had grown to fifty million—that was a 300 percent increase in twenty years. By 1985 it had grown to two hundred forty-seven million, and the 1991 figure was an incredible three hundred ninety-one million. That phenomenal growth makes the Pentecostal Charismatic movement the fastest-growing movement in the world.[12]

Some people have expressed concern when their relatives become involved in a charismatic church, telling them to be careful not to get involved in a "fringe" group. The fact is that charismatics now outnumber the denominations. We have more members than do traditional churches. And we're still growing, while many of the traditional churches are in the process of losing membership. The largest megachurch in almost any American city belongs to the Pentecostal Charismatic movement. All six of the world's largest churches, each with an attendance of fifty thousand or more, are Pentecostal Charismatic churches.[13] We can hardly be identified as a "fringe" group.

I recently read this startling statement: "In all of human history not another nonmilitaristic, nonpolitical volunteer human movement has grown as dramatically as the Pentecostal Charismatic movement in the past twenty-five years."[14] No other movement on earth has ever grown as fast as this movement! God's people in these charismatic churches have certainly laid hold on something powerful.

An American reporter who was visiting Argentina was invited to attend a prayer meeting there. Since it was an all-night prayer meeting in an open field in the winter time, he did not expect to see many people attending. When he got there, he saw twelve thousand exuberant people praying all night long, bringing down strongholds in the heavenlies that would set people free.

The authority God has given us is in a spiritual realm, not just for the purpose of having our needs met or to conquer the problem of the moment. God has given us His authority to bring down the strongholds of the enemy and to establish the kingdom of God in the earth. He wants to take us into that next realm, the "greater-works" realm—that realm that has been promised to a generation that lays hold on God's way and His plan and His anointing for that which He intended us to do.

Eleven

THE "GREATER-WORKS" GENERATION

REALIZING WHAT GOD has done in recent years should give us cause for real hope that we can be the generation He spoke of that will do greater works than our Lord Himself did. Sometimes when we have quoted His promise of our doing greater works, we have left off the last phrase: "because I go unto my Father." It is this phrase that reveals to us the missing link of the power of the promise that Jesus is making.

DISCOVERING THE MISSING LINK TO POWER

> Verily, verily, I say unto you, He that believeth on me, the works that I do shall he do also; and greater works than these shall he do; because I go unto my Father.
> —JOHN 14:12

The reason that we will do greater works is because Jesus has been exalted to the right hand of the Father. Because He returned to the Father as the glorified Christ, He could send the Holy Spirit to us to empower us to do greater works than He did. The apostle Peter revealed this fact to us on the Day of Pentecost when he proclaimed in his sermon: "Therefore being by the right hand of God exalted, and having received of the Father the promise of the Holy Ghost, he hath shed forth this, which ye now see and hear" (Acts 2:33). Though we have received the baptism of the Holy Spirit of which Peter spoke, we have not understood the missing link in our revelation that would inspire faith for the Holy Spirit to now do the greater works through us.

The missing link is this: *The glorified Christ at the right hand of the Father has more to give the church than Jesus did when He was on earth with His disciples.* That is why we can do the works Jesus did, and greater works than those. Earlier I mentioned that Jesus needed to ask the Father to restore to Him the glory that He had before He yielded it up to come to earth and die for our sins (John 17:5). While He was on earth before His death and resurrection, walking with the disciples, Jesus walked as a man, anointed and filled with the Holy Spirit without measure. But He had laid aside the glory He had with the Father before His incarnation.

During His last days on earth, Jesus prayed that the Father would glorify Him with the glory He had with Him before the world was created (John 17:5). The apostle Paul declared: "Who, being in the form of God, thought it not robbery to be equal with God: but made himself of no reputation, and took upon him the form of a servant, and was made in the likeness of men . . . wherefore God also hath highly exalted him, and given him a name which is above every name" (Phil. 2:6–7, 9). Jesus had all this glory with the Father before He came to earth. But to do the work of the incarnate Son, He emptied Himself of His glory. When He was getting ready to return to the Father, He prayed that the Father would restore to Him the glory that He had before the world began.

Jesus knew that when He went to the Father He would regain His former glory, and from that place of majesty by the right hand of the Father, He would send back the Holy Spirit. Jesus told His disciples that the Holy Spirit would teach them things He had not taught them because they could not bear them yet. Jesus knew He had more to give from the right hand of the Father as the glorified Christ than He did as the incarnate Son walking the earth. That is why He said, "It is expedient for you that I go away" (John 16:7).

He told His disciples that He had yet many (imagine what "many" would mean to Jesus) things to say to them, but they could not bear them yet (John 16:12). "Howbeit when he, the Spirit of truth, is come, he will guide you into all truth . . . and he will shew you things to come" (v. 13). The truth is so pure and powerful that it cannot be questioned. It is so powerful that it breaks through the strongholds of our minds and demolishes the lies of the enemy. I love the Spirit of truth. He is not just a truth teller—He is a truth *guide:* He will guide us into all truth, and He will show us things to come. The Holy Spirit will teach us to do the greater works that Jesus said we would do as we allow Him to lead us into all truth.

A. J. Gordon beautifully described the Spirit of the exalted Christ. He wrote:

> Christ at God's right hand will have more to give than the Christ on earth, therefore the church will have more to receive through the Paraclete than through the visible Christ on earth. The Holy Spirit would communicate not the earthly Christ, but the heavenly Christ, reunited with His eternal power, reclothed with the glory He had before the world was, and reendowed with the infinite treasure of grace that was purchased by His death.[1]

We cannot do anything without the Holy Spirit. When we truly understand the vital need we have of the Holy Spirit, we will earnestly desire to cultivate our relationship with Him. As we do, He will release the spirit of the glorified Christ within us with the divine authority Jesus promised us.

When the apostle Paul speaks of Jesus, He refers both to the riches of His grace and the riches of His glory (Eph. 1:7; 3:16). Jesus secured the riches of His grace for us on the cross. He secured the riches of His glory when He ascended and was seated at the right hand of the Father. He is going to pour out both of those riches—grace and glory—on us through the indwelling work of the Holy Spirit.

Jesus said, "All things that the Father hath are mine: therefore said I, that he shall take of mine, and shall shew it unto you" (John 16:15). The Holy Spirit takes the things of Jesus and reveals them to us. As we behold Him, we are changed from glory to glory (2 Cor. 3:18). It is that transforming glory empowering us with the divine nature of God in us that will perform the greater works through us.

Paul understood the exceeding greatness of God's power toward us when he declared that God had set Christ at His own right hand in the "heavenly places, far above all principality, and power, and might, and dominion, and every name that is named, not only in this world, but also in that which is to come" (Eph. 1:20–21). And in another place he wrote, "Who [Christ] . . . is made unto us wisdom, and righteousness, and sanctification, and redemption" (1 Cor. 1:30). It is this majestic authority of the glorified Christ that has been brought to us by the Holy Spirit and is being lived in and through us as we yield to His authority in our lives.

It is the work of the Holy Spirit to teach us of things to come—including the day or hour when the Son of man would come (John 16:13). Jesus said, "Of that day and that hour knoweth no man, no, not the angels which are in heaven, neither the Son, but the Father" (Mark 13:32). A more accurate rendering of "neither the Son" in the Greek language is "not yet the Son." But there came a time after Jesus ascended to heaven when He poured out revelation of things to come through the Holy Spirit. He revealed to the apostle Paul His plan for the church that He had not revealed when He walked the earth. And to the apostle John exiled on the isle of Patmos, He opened the visions of the Book of Revelation. Though the Canon of Scripture is the complete revelation of God's Word to us, we are not yet walking in as complete an understanding of that Word as we are going to walk in as we allow the Holy Spirit to teach us and bring us into relationship with the living Word.

If we are to be a part of the greater-works generation, then it is imperative that we cultivate our relationship with the Holy Spirit, yielding our members to Him to become His servants (Rom. 6:19). The church is the embodiment of the Holy Spirit, providing the tabernacle for His presence. The Holy Spirit is going to return to the Father one day—in the church—His body on the earth. Christ is going to be manifested to the world through His glorious church without spot or wrinkle.

There is going to be a people living when Jesus returns who will do the greater works Jesus promised. I believe we are living in that generation. I don't believe any generation since the one living when Christ ascended into heaven has done the greater works to which He referred. I think that generation—the Acts-of-the-Apostles' generation—experienced these greater works. But then the church passed through the Dark Ages and lost so much of the truth. That precious truth has been restored to her through the centuries and is now being restored to her in fuller revelation, which is going to make the greater works Jesus promised possible again. The wonderful truths that are presently being restored to the church will make it possible for us to do the "greater works" Jesus intended for us to do.

EMPOWERED THROUGH RELATIONSHIP

JOHN THE BELOVED seemingly enjoyed the most intimate relationship with Jesus of all the disciples, reclining on His bosom as they ate. The Scriptures are clear concerning the fact that Jesus had more intimate relationships with certain people than He did with others. This was true even among His disciples. Among the twelve, there were the three—Peter,

James, and John—who were often separated out to accompany Him to the Mount of Transfiguration, for example, or to pray with Him in Gethsemane.

But it was John who earned the title "the Beloved" because of his intimate relationship with the Master. All we have to do is to read his Gospel and his epistles to see the depth of understanding and love that his heart had responded to as he abandoned himself to this relationship. John understood the divinity of Christ perhaps more clearly than any of the other Gospel writers.

From his writings, it is hard to remember John's beginnings as a son of thunder (Mark 3:17). God had sanctified that capacity to "thunder," filling him with His love, and then allowed him to hear the thunder of God on the isle of Patmos as Jesus Himself revealed to John things that were to come. From this beloved disciple we learn most about the living Word and how He is manifested to men. Reading the fourteenth, fifteenth, and sixteenth chapters of the Gospel of John every day for a month, I am convinced, would change our lives completely. Meditating on them and letting the Holy Spirit teach us would result in a great unveiling of the work of the Holy Spirit as promised to every believer.

John began his Gospel by declaring: "In the beginning was the Word, and the Word was with God, and the Word was God" (John 1:1). There was no manger for John, no Bethlehem or shepherds or wise men. That was incidental to the true account of the incarnate Word of God. John declares: "All things were made by him; and without him was not any thing made that was made" (John 1:3). John understood some things about this living Word made flesh that others did not. He declared: "And we beheld his glory, the glory as of the only begotten of the Father" (John 1:14). His eyes were opened to the true divinity of Christ. That is the vision of Jesus that the Holy Spirit wants to give to us.

Not only did John have a revelation of Christ as the living Word, he knew as well how Jesus would manifest Himself to men. He quotes Jesus' words: "He that hath my commandments, and keepeth them, he it is that loveth me: and he that loveth me shall be loved of my Father, and I will love him, and will manifest myself to him" (John 14:21). When Jesus used the word *manifest* here, He was saying, "I will allow Myself to be intimately known and understood by another. I will tell him things that others do not know who do not keep My commandments." Jesus promised to reveal His love and the love of the Father to those who kept His commandments.

In John's epistle, he speaks of "that which was from the beginning, which we have heard, which we have seen with our eyes, which we have looked upon, and our hands have handled, of the Word of life" (1 John 1:1). He had entered into the reality of the eternal life manifested through the Son of God and the fellowship with the Father and with his Son Jesus Christ (1 John 1:2). And He recorded it by the power of the Holy Spirit so that we might enter the reality of that empowering relationship as well.

THE THRESHOLD OF THE IMPOSSIBLE

AS WE BEGIN to walk in this revelation of Christ, we will come to faith to believe Him to do the greater works in us and through us that He has promised to do. As we choose to believe His Word and walk in obedience to His will, our lives will become temples filled with the Holy Ghost who will pour His divine power through us in answer to life's impossible situations. Then Jesus' Great Commission will begin to seem reasonable to us: "Go ye into all the world, and preach the gospel to every creature. . . . And these signs shall follow them that believe; in my name shall they cast out devils; they shall speak with new tongues; they shall take up serpents; and if they drink any deadly thing, it shall not hurt them; they shall lay hands on the sick, and they shall recover" (Mark 16:15, 17–18).

Have you ever considered raising someone from the dead?

Does that seem impossible? To man's natural mind, yes. But to the mind renewed by the Spirit of God and walking in obedience to His will, it is not only possible, but it is a current happening in the ministries of some. There are men of God today who have raised people from the dead. Benson Idahosa has raised eight people from the dead in the last few years.[2] And Mahesh Chavda's healing ministry began when he prayed for a young boy in Africa, and he was raised from the dead.[3]

Dr. Sam Sasser told the story of his friend from the Marshall Islands, Emtee Batumah, who raised a person from the dead during the 1960s. The person was already in her funeral box—not a coffin as we know, but a very cheap box. This Marshallese man was a spiritual wild man. He was attending the woman's funeral and marched to the front where the box was, where he began to laugh aloud hilariously. As the congregation sang, "When the Roll Is Called Up Yonder," Emtee Batumah stood in front of the coffin and disrupted the service with his laughter. He was laughing because the Spirit of God began to speak to him, and he saw what God wanted to do. He laughed and laughed. Finally, he quit laughing, went over to the woman in the box, and shouted, "Get out of the box!"

Can't you see it now, this precious brother who is supposed to say a few words of eulogy over the deceased instead begins to laugh hilariously, and then says to the corpse, "Get out of the box!" Well, she didn't do anything—she was dead, you know. So he started laughing again; he just threw his head back and continued to laugh. Still nothing happened. The third time he went over to her he picked her up by the hair of the head and shouted emphatically, "I said, get out of the box!"

When he did that, the woman sat up, looked around, and began to get out of the box. The Marshallese people were so astounded they shrieked and ran out of the building, some of them jumping through windows to get out. That miracle resulted in a revival movement in the entire nation of the Marshall Islands. Thousands were converted and trained in the Bible school that Dr. Sasser established there. Today, the leaders—president, governors, and senators—of those islands are men who have been trained in Dr. Sasser's school, and they came personally to greet him when he revisited the Marshall Islands.

Who is going to do these greater works? Is it just Emtee Batumah? Is it just Benson Idahosa? Is it just Mahesh Chavda? Or is it possible that one of these days Sarah Smith and Sam Jones are going to do them? I believe the answer is *yes*. These miracles will happen when we embrace the revelation of the Holy Ghost in the Scriptures rather than what the theologians say, the excuses of the higher critical group, or even what some charismatic teacher has said unless it is anointed in the truth of revelation of what Jesus meant when He said it. The Holy Spirit will keep revealing what Jesus is saying. I believe the Holy Spirit is saying to our generation, "Now it's time to walk in the authority you have been given."

Evan Roberts, that great Welsh revivalist, said this simple thing: "Revival is knowing the Holy Spirit and cooperating with Him." The Holy Spirit has a way by which He works; He has things that He teaches; He has revelation to give; He has the plan of God; and He will speak it to us if our hearts are open, willing, and obedient.

The church has had to have some pruning done in our lives to open our eyes and our ears to the revelation of Jesus through the Holy Spirit. We have been choosing to keep His commandments and to come into relationship with the Father and the Son through the Holy Spirit. Our priorities have been changing from being absorbed with "our ministry" and personal success to a love relationship with Jesus. The foundations of righteousness are being laid in our lives through the Word so that we can receive revelation and understand what God was saying.

I believe the prayer of the apostle Paul is being answered today:

That the God of our Lord Jesus Christ, the Father of glory, may give unto you the spirit of wisdom and revelation in the knowledge of him: the eyes of your understanding being enlightened; that ye may know what is the hope of his calling, and what the riches of the glory of his inheritance in the saints, and what is the exceeding greatness of his power to us-ward who believe.

—EPHESIANS 1:17–19

We are beginning to walk in the spirit of wisdom and revelation in knowing our God—the living Word. And we are going to know the riches of the His glory and the greatness of His power working in us and through us.

Twelve

The Breakthrough Generation

For a number of years the church has been confessing more than she possesses. Now it is time for a breakthrough into the reality of the authority Christ promised us. Before any great move of God can occur, there must first come revelation mixed with a faith that enables us to walk in the fresh revelation. Those who step into that walk are the ones who are involved in the breakthrough process. They will experience divine empowerings for things that have not been attempted before. They will be bold because of the faith in their hearts, ignited by the fresh revelation they have received from God. His Word has come alive to them, and a fire is burning in their hearts.

Theology of Victory

I believe God is giving a breakthrough word on authority that will launch a new generation willing to enforce His victory in His name. They will do the unheard of and the unthinkable. They will not follow in the prevailing theology of powerlessness. They will develop a theology of victory that will bring glory to God. This time God will be seen as great in power, and Satan will take his rightful place of defeat.

We are rejoicing that in our local area, for the first time, a number of pastors have joined together to believe God for a breakthrough into the harvest. Never before have we talked of praying together for God to give us, not just souls, but our entire city. For the past year we have been praying regularly in concerts of prayer that God would bless every pastor and every church in our city with revival.

LOCAL CONCERTS OF PRAYER

GOD BEGAN TO speak to my heart about starting a concert of prayer in our local area, Tri-Cities, Tennessee. My heart was stirred with what I was reading about cities being won for God in other countries. "Why should we just sit and read about what God is doing in Argentina and other nations?" I asked myself earnestly.

I appealed to our local fellowship of ministers who meet monthly for prayer and fellowship, sharing with them two biblical patterns for "concerts of prayer" to take our cities for God. As I shared these principles with them, they became convinced that we could gather pastors and pray until the heavens would open in our area for God to bring in a great harvest of souls.

The scriptural basis for our venture was twofold: first, the example of Paul as he called the church together at Ephesus (Acts 20:17). Notice that the apostle did not call the *churches,* but the *church,* at Ephesus to come together. Pastors of various groups within the city of Ephesus saw themselves as elders of the church of Ephesus, not of individual churches in the city. This understanding of a regional church is very important, because if pastors can see themselves working together to build the church in their city or region (no matter how many local expressions of that church there are), they can establish spiritual unity.

That understanding of spiritual unity leads us to the second scriptural basis for our venture: "There the LORD commanded the blessing, even life for evermore" (Ps. 133:3). Only as we cultivate this spiritual unity of building the regional church in our area can we expect the blessing of life that God wants to give as we pray for our cities. It became clear to us that if we could come into true unity as pastors and cultivate that unity in our congregations, God would command His blessing in our midst. And no one can keep a blessing back that God commands. If pastors will give themselves to this vision of unity and begin praying together regularly, once a month, and then even weekly, they will begin to see breakthroughs in their community.

The greatest battle to be won is the one against Satan's lie that it will never happen—that the pastors of your area will never be willing to gather together. And even if they did, they would never be united in prayer for the city. It is in this battle that we have to exercise our faith. In that way spiritual authority will be released for your city. The pastors of our area have come together in unity. They are praying for our area, establishing a covering of intercession over our whole region as we take our positions as leaders—the spiritual gatekeepers—of our cities.

The apostle Paul's exhortation to Timothy regarding supplications, prayers, intercessions, and giving of thanks for all men strengthens our resolve to win our city for God (1 Tim. 2:1). The reason the apostle gives for this earnest prayer is, "This is good and acceptable in the sight of God our Saviour; who will have all men to be saved, and to come unto the knowledge of the truth" (1 Tim. 2:3–4). In this passage, Paul exhorts us to pray for everyone in a region because God wishes all men to be saved.

Paul does not present this message as a promotional prayer program, but as a lifestyle. The church is mobilized through prayer to be the spiritual gatekeepers in the heavenly places over the city. Prayer evangelism is reaching every person and bringing every household in touch with the power and love of God through prayer. It is the whole church reaching the whole city with the gospel through prayer.

PRAYER EVANGELISM

A FRESH CONCEPT of evangelism, called "prayer evangelism," is being shared in the body of Christ today, bringing together the *pray-ers* and the *soul winners* in a biblical balance. The tendency of believers to polarize their identities as worshipers and pray-ers at one end and at the other as evangelists and soul winners reveals the religious strongholds of our minds that have kept the church from reaping the harvest. Nowhere do the Scriptures teach that we are to be either a pray-er and worshiper or an evangelist and soul winner. Jesus' commission to preach the gospel and make disciples was made to everyone who would follow Him. In that same way, the Scriptures teach that everyone should give themselves continually to prayer.

PRAYING FOR OUR CITIES

GOD CARES ABOUT cities. He sent the prophet Jonah to rescue Ninevah from destruction. Jesus wept over Jerusalem. He spoke woes over Bethsaida and Capernaum by name for their refusal to repent. We must release our faith for our cities and take our authority over the work of the enemy to rescue them for God.

The Argentine church has laid hold of the concept of prayer evangelism for entire cities and have seen astounding results. Ed Silvoso has proven the effectiveness of this approach using the city of Resistencia as the first laboratory for the implementation of these principles. Based on the biblical principles of unity among pastors, reconciliation, and extraordinary prayer, the entire city was reached. The result was an unheard of 102 percent growth in church attendance during the three-year period of 1988 to 1991! Thousands of pastors and leaders in hundreds of congregations are impacting cities around the world through prayer evangelism.[1] Through their unity of purpose, they are reaping the harvest on a much larger scale than ever before. As we choose to experience the wonder of unity as God has intended, we will begin to walk in the works in which Christ has foreordained that we walk.

Jesus told His disciples that they would do greater works than He did, because He went to the Father. This glorified Christ empowered them through the Holy Spirit, and they turned their world upside down, evangelizing the entire known world in a few years.

I believe we are living in the "greater-works" generation today that will walk in all that Jesus bought for us by returning to the Father. The harvest we can anticipate will involve entire cities and people groups turning to God because of the unity and authority in which we, the church of Jesus Christ, will walk, releasing the power of God to bring men and women to salvation. In the face of the wonderful reports we are receiving of God's harvest being reaped in other places, each of us must accept the challenge to become a part of this End-Time revival and great harvest of souls for our "worlds." In this way we can bring glory to God in the earth and fulfill His wonderful purpose for our own lives as well.

NOTES

CHAPTER ONE
REVELATION OF AUTHORITY

1. Dick Eastman, *The Jericho Hour* (Lake Mary, FL: Creation House, 1994), 7.
2. C. Peter Wagner, *Crest of the Wave* (Ventura, CA: Regal Books, 1983), 25.
3. Mission Frontiers Vision Brochure, vol. 12, nos. 1 and 2, U.S. Center for World Missions, Pasadena, California (January/February 1990), 3.
4. Johannes Fascius, *The Powerhouse of God* (Tonbridge, Kent, ENGLAND: Sovereign World, Ltd., 1995), 53.
5. C. Peter Wagner, *Engaging the Enemy* (Ventura, CA: Regal Books, 1991), 110.
6. Mission Frontiers Brochure, 4.
7. Mission Frontiers Vision Brochure, no. 7, (May/June 1993), 6.
8. Wagner, *Engaging the Enemy*, 110.

CHAPTER TWO
AUTHORITY OF THE GREAT COMMISSION

1. From information from the International Institute, Buenos Aires, Argentina, 1994.
2. Wagner, *Engaging the Enemy,* 110.

CHAPTER THREE
THE PATTERN SON: ESTABLISHING THE PATTERN

1. Wagner, *Engaging the Enemy*, 83–92.

CHAPTER FIVE
RECOGNIZING THE DEVIL'S DEFEAT

1. Edward Silvoso, *That None Should Perish* (Ventura, CA: Regal Books, 1995), 178.
2. Ibid., 197.
3. William Gurnall, *The Christian in Full Armor* (England: Banner of Truth Trust, 1655, 1989), 115; and S. D. Gordon, *Quiet Talks About the Tempter* (New York: Fleming H. Revell Co., 1910).
4. Gurnall, *The Christian in Full Armor,* 115.
5. Ibid., 114–115.
6. Harold Caballeros is a Guatemalan pastor and was a speaker at the First Global Conference on Prayer Evangelism, November 15–18, 1995, Los Angeles, California.

Notes

Chapter Six
Breakthrough Keys

1. From a message by Dick Eastman given at the First Global Conference on Prayer Evangelism, November 15–18, 1995, Los Angeles, California.

Chapter Ten
Releasing the Authority

1. Dick Eastman, *The Jericho Hour*, 22.
2. Taken from an article written by Dr. Ralph Winter, U.S. Center for World Mission, Pasadena, California (April 1997).
3. C. Peter Wagner, *Warfare Prayer* (Ventura, CA: Regal Books, 1992), 120.
4. From a message by Edward Silvoso given at the First Global Conference on Prayer Evangelism, November 15–18, 1995, Los Angeles, California.
5. Mission Frontiers Vision Brochure (July/August 1993), 12.
6. Ibid., 14.
7. Ibid., 15.
8. Mission Frontiers Vision Brochure (May/June 1993), 6.
9. Religion Report, n.d., n.p.
10. Religion Report, vol. 9, no. 1 (December 26, 1994), 1.
11. Taken from an article by Luis Bush titled "The Unfinished Task," published by Mission Frontiers.
12. Wagner, *Warfare Prayer*, 47.
13. Ibid., 48.
14. Ibid., 47.

Chapter Eleven
The "Greater-Works" Generation

1. A. J. Gordon, *The Ministry of the Holy Spirit* (Fort Lauderdale, FL: Editorial CLIE, n.d.).
2. From a message by Benson Idahosa, given at the Third World Believer's Summit '93, August 15–21, 1993, Nassau, Bahamas.
3. Mahesh Chavda, *Only Love Can Make a Miracle* (Ann Arbor, MI: Servant Publications, 1990), 14–16.

Chapter Twelve
The Breakthrough Generation

1. From a message by Ed Silvoso given at the First Global Conference on Prayer Evangelism, November 15–18, 1995, Los Angeles, California.

BOOKS BY SUE CURRAN

The Praying Church
Principles and Power of Corporate Prayer
A sovereign revival released the keys of corporate prayer to a pastor and a congregation. This book is written as a result of that revelation. It has been translated into several languages and has become an international handbook on corporate prayer.

The Joshua Generation
Winning Your Children for Kingdom Purposes
This book conveys in conversational style biblical principles that have proven successful for raising children. It will show you how to give your children a sense of destiny and purpose.

The Forgiving Church
Offering a stunning portrait of the key of forgiveness within the church, this book gives practical strategies for answering God's call to become a forgiving church, the foundational position for revival.

Kingdom Principles
Basics to Kingdom Living
Delineating the basic scriptural principles on which Shekinah Church was founded, *Kingdom Principles* serves as a Christian text and training manual around the world. It has been translated for international distribution.

Excellence in Leadership
This book deals with the subjects of character, leadership development, understanding leadership, and principles of growth. It is used as a manual in leadership training conferences.

Tapes Available From Sue Curran

*The following list is a sampling
of tape series titles available:*

- Our Authority Over Satan
- From Victim to Victor
- Devil-Proof Your Life
- Free Indeed
- Your Seed Gift
- Setting Captives Free
- Releasing the Anointing
- Revival: Filled With God
- The Fervent Prayer

**A catalog with a complete listing of audio tapes is
available through Shekinah Church at:**

Shekinah Church Ministries
394 Glory Road
Blountville, TN 37617
Phone: 423.323.2242
Fax: 423.279.7132
E-mail: shekinah@usit.net